Our Precious Holy Bible

A Series of Lessons
On the origin
of
The King James Bible

Our

Precious

Holy Bible

By

R. M. Timmons

Our Precious Holy Bible
By Ryan Timmons
Copyright 2006 ©

Printed in the United States of America

Published by:

R. M. Timmons
509 E. Jefferson St.
Goshen, IN 46528
(574) 534-7170
Email: thedivinelibrary@gmail.com

For additional copies write or call

First Printing 2006
Second Printing 2007
Third Printing 2009

DEDICATION:

Dedicated to the Adult Sunday School Class of
Trinity Holiness Tabernacle:

As insufficient as it may be, I present to you
This meager offering
With the hopes that you would be
Strengthened in your personal commitment to God's
Word
And that you might use these studies to
Convince the gainsayers.

CONTENTS:

FOREWARD

Several years ago as I walked into a Christian bookstore I was taken aback by something that seemed to come out of no-where. Being just an average boy raised in a solid conservative church I knew of no other Bible than the King James Version. My parents read that Bible in our home. Our pastor used the KJV in his preaching on Sundays and in our Bible studies during the midweek services. Our memory verses were from the King James Version. In fact, that was the version used by the curriculum in our Sunday School for as long as I could remember. It was by far the most popular English version, and I had not been familiar with any other with the exception of the para-phrased best-seller of the early 1970's called The Living Bible – and my earliest recollection of this was in the form of a chil-dren's Bible, so I personally viewed it as more of a "story book" than an authoritative translation of God's Word.

What stunned me upon entering that Christian bookstore back in the late 1980s were the signs hung throughout the store that blatantly stated *"If King James were alive today, he would read the NIV!"* My initial reaction was stunned irritation in my heart in defense of what I had always been raised to respect and hold so dear. I felt as though the very Bible I had grown to love was being undermined and had come under attack by a marketing scheme to be replaced, as though, like so many other things we own, it needed to be upgraded or improved. I was shocked. I became angry! It was such a violation of one of my core values. Since then, there have been countless modern versions, as if the floodgates have been opened and anything that floats down-stream has been free to call itself a "Bible" claiming authority as the word of God.

Did I overreact? Are these modern versions really a prob-lem, or am I simply an obstinate legalist who needs to *chill out*? There is one major thing that causes me to lean more conserva-tive on issues such as this. My concerns are demonstrated in the response of Pilate in the presence of Jesus, the true *living* Word. All appeared to be business as usual as he tried the One standing before him that fateful morning. Apparently a radical religious leader had stirred up some trouble and made a bunch of people really mad... mad enough to want to kill him, but they needed Pilate's assistance to make the whole plan legal. This *circus* of a trial took an abrupt change when he discovered that the One accused made the claim He is Deity! *Yes, this lowly Nazarene carpenter-turned-preacher claims to be the Son of God!* This claim forced Pilate to put more serious thought into his decision as the crowd ruthlessly pressured him. History records his fatal decision, and tradition reveals a life of dreadful regret.

How does this relate to my sentiment and convictions concerning the King James Bible? Well, it comes from a similar claim. **The Bible itself claims to be the Word of God.** 2 Timothy 3:16-17 says, *"All scripture is given by inspiration of God, and is profitable for doctrine, for reproof, for correction, for instruction in righteousness: That the man of God may be perfect, throughly furnished unto all good works."* Based upon this assertion **it further claims an exceptional power**. Being *"sharper than any twoedged sword,"* God's all-penetrating Word is a discerner of not only our thoughts, but the very intentions of our heart (Hebrews 4:13). With claims such as these we should certainly give the more earnest consideration in what we set in place before our families as a sure and safe guide for our eternal souls.

Having been written during both war and times of peace, from the deepest valleys of despair to the highest pinnacles of rejoicing, this compilation of 66 books is extraordinary in the physical facts alone. No other book or set of books can make the same claims. Over 40 different men, from kings to mere peasants, statesmen, scholars and fishermen throughout 40 generations spanning over 1,500 years, writing in the wilderness, and in the palace and despicable ancient prison cells, wrote as they were inspired by the Holy Ghost. Yet there is an undeniable continuity that would not be possible were it not God-breathed. Though not a book of history alone, that which is recorded in the first eleven chapters of the Bible (Genesis 1-11), lays out a logical, holy foundation for a sound and trustworthy Christian worldview. Our understanding and faith in the beginning of all things as told to us by the only One who witnessed it all provides the answers to all the issues facing mankind today. What a wonderful gift given to man from God – the *written* Word revealing the *living* Word, Jesus Christ the Son of God, and God the Son, Savior of all who will believe!

Our adult Sunday School class was genuinely blessed by the hours of study and weeks of teaching resulting in this printed work. The topic is one not so quickly tackled by most, however Brother Ryan felt the burden and labored to pass his passion along to us. A very capable teacher and preacher, his study and gathering of material in defense of the King James Version of the Bible is a worthy contribution for a subject of such infinite value... *God's* Word; *Our Precious Holy Bible.* I echo the words of another in saying, "Read it to be wise, believe it to be safe, and practice it to be right."

Michael A. Johnson, pastor
Trinity Holiness Tabernacle

PREFACE

The Scriptures, in Proverbs 23:23 exhort us to "Buy the truth and sell it not..." As holiness people we must guard our doctrines and theology. We are what we believe. That is why our doctrines and theology are important. Our doctrines and theology shape our beliefs about God and allow us to have a correct understanding of Him. Where do we receive our doctrines and theology? We receive them from God's book. Therefore it is of the utmost importance that we have the right version. If we are using a 'bible' that has been perverted or corrupted by man's vain philosophies then our perception of God will be perverted or corrupted and our theology will not be correct, therefore we will not live right before a Holy God. WE ARE WHAT WE BELIEVE. It is imperative to have a proper view about God in order to live the way He wants us to live.

In our day we are witnessing a great falling away from the fundamental truths of holiness and righteousness that have always been a trademark of God's true children. I believe that this is a direct result of Satan's scheme to undermine the Word of God. He has done so by flooding the marketplace with hundreds of counterfeits that are propagated and endorsed by 'scholars' that are antagonistic to the King James Bible. The sad fact is that the multitudes of people, who ignorantly consult these corrupted versions, believe a lie - the same lie that Satan proposed at the beginning of man's fall from God. "Ye will be as gods". Satan was suggesting that they would be wiser and more enlightened. But we are able to see the devastating effects of this lie by witnessing the church-world being entangled in a web of carnality and deceit. Unless the grace of God rescues them they will be deceived all the way to the gates of hell!

We, who believe in the steadfast Truth contained in the King James Bible, have a firm foundation that will not falter. We have the pure Word of God to give us proper theology and doctrine. Having said this, "We ought to give the MORE EARNEST HEED to the things that we have heard, lest at any time we should let them slip (Heb. 2:1). We, who believe in the authority of the King James Bible, will not be saved by that belief alone. If the King James Bible is the True Word of God then we should live according to its commands, precepts, and promises. Woe unto us if we do not heed them! We will receive the greater damnation because we had in our possession the Words of Truth and did not profit by them. It is a dreadful thought to consider that such responsibility has been placed upon us. In the midst of the confusion surrounding the exclusiveness of the King James Bible we must never forget our Lord Jesus Christ has promised to preserve the Words of God (**Matt 24:35** **"Heaven and earth shall pass away, BUT MY WORDS SHALL NOT PASS AWAY."**) Not only is He able to preserve the Word of God, but He is able to preserve us to its keeping (**Jude 24 "Now unto Him that IS ABLE TO KEEP YOU FROM FALLING, and to present you faultless before the presence of His glory with exceeding joy..."**).

These studies, originally given to the Adult Sunday School class at Trinity Holiness Tabernacle, have been condensed, in order that the basic principles of the lessons may be remembered by those who attended. Hopefully they will be useful to you for personal edification or as a tool to help point a wayward believer into greater truth. It is my prayer that the studies contained herein will help to increase your confidence in the King James Bible's superiority over modern versions and cause you to cherish God's Words.

Your servant for Christ's sake,
R. M. Timmons
2006

Chapter 1
The Preciousness of The Holy Bible

Our Precious Holy Bible
1 Samuel 3:1

And **the child Samuel ministered unto the LORD before Eli.**
And the word of the LORD was precious **in those days; there
was no open vision.** *I Samuel 3:1*

T he text that we have chosen as a springboard for
our lessons is found in First Samuel. Although the
main context of this chapter is describing God's call to young
Samuel, this first verse reveals some very important information about the spiritual condition of Israel at that time. The Bible says "the word of the LORD was precious in those days."
The fact that the Word was called 'precious' does not necessar-
ily mean that the people of that day thought so highly of God's
Word that they cherished it like a valuable treasure. No, the
exact opposite is implied. The people did not cherish God's
Word, therefore God had withdrawn Himself from them and it
was a rare occasion when God chose to speak. This will help to
explain my first point in describing the 'preciousness of God's
Word'.

I. God's Word is RARE
The Hebrew word for 'precious' in the text mentioned above
means 'rare'. It was a rare occasion when God spoke. It was

17

rare for God to choose a man to reveal His plans to. It was rare for God to open the curtain of His sovereign will and allow men to peer into the heavenly realms where they could behold and briefly understand the mind of God. The obscurity of God's Word may be hard for Americans to comprehend because they reside in the one of the freest countries on the face of this earth. As Americans, we have the privilege of living in a nation which was founded upon God's Word and because of God's Word. From that time until the present our culture has been surrounded by the Bible. If a sinner desires a Word from God they don't have to go far to get it. They could simply go rummaging through the stuff that they have accumulated from the time they were a child. If they would do so, they would find a small Gideon's New Testament Bible that was handed to them in grade school. They would also possibly find a Bible presented to them by their grandma or grandpa when they were young. If none can be found anywhere in the house they could find the nearest secular or Christian bookstore and purchase one there. If they could not afford to buy the leather-bound editions they could go to the nearest Goodwill store and purchase one for a dollar. If they could not afford a dollar they could ask many of us who have numerous copies in our possession and we could give them one. How many copies of the Bible do you have in your home? It certainly would not be considered a rare commodity. You may not have a hidden treasure-chest full of gold or costly gems that men may consider to be so precious and rare, but if you have a Holy Bible you have something that is far more valuable.

II. God's Word is VALUABLE

We have another text which further elaborates this idea of the preciousness of God's Word. **II Peter 1:4 says "Whereby are given unto us exceeding great and _precious_ promises."** The promises found in God's Word are precious. Notice it is not just a promise (singular), but promises (plural). They are not considered a rarity because they are too numerous to count. The fact of the matter is that when we have a large amount of something we tend to take it for granted. There are numerous promises in the Bible, but to us who are children of the King they are exceedingly great and PRECIOUS. That is why we

consider them to be very VALUABLE. **Psalm 119:72, 127 says"
The law of Thy mouth is <u>better</u> unto me than <u>thousands</u> of
gold and silver. Therefore I love Thy commandments above
gold; yea, above fine gold."** David, the king who had wealth
beyond measure, who, no doubt, wore a crown of gold upon
his forehead and had clothing weaved with golden threads
knew that the value of God's Word far exceeded that of his
earthly riches.

III. God's Word is COSTLY

The word 'precious' in some instances means 'rare' and
'valuable', but it also means 'costly'. There are some things in
your house that you would sell to me if I made you a reason-
able offer. There may even be some things that you would pay
me to take. You may also have some special heirlooms that
although, they may not have cost too much to buy they are so
precious to you that you would not take any amount of money
for them. **Proverbs 20:15 says "There is gold, and a multitude
of rubies: but the lips of knowledge are a *precious* jewel."**
"Precious" means "costly". If you were to lose one of those
valuable heirlooms or have it stolen you would pay any
amount to retrieve it. From God's lips precede knowledge that
is more valuable than <u>anything</u> money can buy. Think of it! –
We realize the value of money. We know that it helps us to
purchase the things that we want and need. We realize the
value of our job which allows us to make money. But it is the
<u>knowledge</u> that helps us to do our job and to be able to do it as
'unto the Lord' is more valuable than the money or the job. I
don't think we will ever fully realize how costly the Word's of
God are. The people were astonished at the doctrine of Christ
and recognized that there was something special about His
Words. They said **"He speaks as one having authority" (Mk.
1:22).** We see that Christ had these precious lips of knowledge.
Jesus said **"the words that I speak unto you, they are spirit,
and they are life" (Jn. 6:63).** Peter said **"Lord, to whom shall
we go: thou hast the words of eternal life" (Jn. 6:68).**

John 7:46 says "Never man spake like this man." This was
the only reply that the officers could give after they heard
Christ speak. Never a man spoke like the Lord Jesus Christ.
He spoke and the worlds were created. He spoke and the de-

mons were cast out. He spoke and the lame were healed. **"He sent His Word and healed them" (Ps 107:20).** JUST A WORD! Just one Word from the Master is all it takes. God's Word is precious and I hope that we are able to realize the value of it. This series of lessons is intended to help us realize the costliness of the Holy Bible. We should cherish it above everything else because God does, for He says in **Psalm 138:2 "Thou hast magnified THY WORD above all Thy name."**

CHAPTER 2
WHY IS THE HOLY BIBLE SO PRECIOUS?

We have just established the fact that the Holy Bible is precious, but now we must ask the question "Why is it so precious?" It is precious because it contains the Words of Almighty God. The eternal, pure, and true Word of God. Why is the Bible so precious? Because it reveals the fact that God desired to speak to mankind. What if God had never spoken? What if He had never decided to reveal Himself? To consider the implications of this proposition is horrifying.

It is impossible to know God unless He reveals Himself to us **(Lk. 10:22)**. Now, I would like to look at 3 basic ways that God speaks to mankind to reveal Himself.

I. God Speaks Through Our SURROUNDINGS (*The Creation*).

Psalm 19:1-3 says "The heavens *DECLARE* the glory of God; and the firmament sheweth His handiwork. Day unto day *UTTERETH SPEECH*, and night unto night sheweth knowledge. There is no *SPEECH* nor *LANGUAGE* where their *VOICE* is not heard."

Hebrews 11:3 says "Through faith we understand that the worlds were framed by the *WORD OF GOD...*"

Everywhere you look in the universe you can learn something about God. He is speaking through His creation. He is conveying a message. The sad thing is that people do not hear His speech and often misinterpret His messages. David said **"When I <u>CONSIDER</u> Thy heavens, the work of Thy fingers, the moon and the stars, which thou hast ordained; What is man that thou art mindful of him? And the son of man that thou visitest him? (Ps. 8:3, 4).** Let us take a moment to consider some things about God's creation. Consider our solar system. The earth, which is one of the smallest bodies, is simply one small part of a vast universe. We are told that there are galaxies and solar systems beyond ours. It seemingly goes on forever. Our solar system is constructed in such a way that there is perfect harmony between the planets. Imagine if there were no sun or moon. Without these there would be no life on earth. Consider the position of the earth in its relation to the sun. If it were only a few degrees closer we would all burst into flames. If we would happen to move a few degrees away we would be frozen. How does it all stay perfectly synchronized?

The entire creation speaks of a Wisdom that far surpasses our finite minds. What is the universe saying about God? It says He is Omnipotent, He is Omniscient, and He is a good God. As a child I would look up into the midnight sky and something was telling me that I was small. Something was telling me that there was Someone much greater than me 'up there'. When I see photographs of space and how the blackness goes on for infinity it tells me there is an eternity. Scientists have never found a "dead end road" in space and neither does the spirit of man have an abrupt end. There is an eternity.

So far, earth has been the only planet to contain life. That tells me God's love is exclusive. I do not believe that there are other 'earths' or alien life forms on other planets because the Bible says **"God so loved <u>the world</u> (Jn. 3:16)"**, not worlds (plural). Jesus died for the sins of the whole world, not the universe. He died once. He did not have many crosses on many planets. He gave His precious life one time. That tells me how much God truly loved us.

Now, let us leave the universe for a moment and focus our attention upon the creation around us. We will now exchange a telescope for a microscope. A microscope can reveal to us the intricacies of the creation. Microscopic animals, molecules, and atoms reveal the fact that God is precise in His work. He is concerned about details. Think of the attention and work that goes into carving each individual snowflake and they are all distinct one from the other yet they melt in an instant. Why would God make them so detailed? Consider all of God's creation and how skillfully he put things together. Consider His greatest work – man. We are fearfully and wonderfully made! And yet we have barely scratched the surface of all the things that God is speaking through His creation.

II. God Speaks Through His SON (The Christ)
John 1:1-3 says "In the beginning was THE WORD, and the Word was with God, and the Word was God." The same was in the beginning with God.
Hebrews 1:1,2 God, who at sundry times and in divers manners spake in time past unto the fathers by the prophets, Hath in these last days SPOKEN unto us by HIS SON, ...

God has spoken the greatest words of love that mankind could ever hear through His Son, Jesus Christ. Everything that God ever wanted to say to mankind He was able to say in one word – JESUS. We would often consider 'the Word' to be that which we have written down for us to read, but there is another aspect of 'the Word'. There is the written Word and the Living Word. **Revelation 19:13 says "He was clothed with a vesture dipped in blood, and *His Name is called The Word of God"*.** This verse is speaking about Jesus Christ the Son of God. In this verse He is given the title "The Word of God". The Apostle John in his gospel writes about "The Word". He attributes this title to Jesus Christ.

The Greek definition of this title is a word with deep significance in Greek literature. It is called the "Logos". It is a philosophical word. It does not simply describe a word that is written or spoken. It is not simply a set of letters arranged in such a way as to create what we call a "word". It meant the inward thought or reason behind a word. To the Greek philosopher who did not believe in the One True God, yet acknowledged the existence of a greater organized power, this word meant 'the mind or reason on which the whole order of the universe depends'. It is a complex theory to describe, so let me try to simplify it.

You may have read or written a few love letters in your life-time. The one who writes the love letter puts the words on the paper with such delicate care. There is feeling behind every letter. The emotions of the writer flow through the pen and those emotions translate into words. The loved one who reads the letter can feel the words as if they came straight from the heart of their lover. Anyone else who would happen to read this letter may not be affected, but to those whose souls have been connected by love can sense the person behind the words. The love letter consists of more than just words on a page. There are intentions behind the words. This Greek word "Logos" is the opposite of thoughtlessness or rashness. It is a reasoned word that is spoken with varied intents behind it. It means "the thought behind the word".

A word is also a means of communication. It is with words that we establish a connection between ourselves and other people. In the Bible we see God desiring to make a connection with man by communicating with him. God speaks words. In the Old Testament, God spoke through the prophets. They would stand and proclaim their message with the words **"Thus Saith the LORD"**. In the New Testament God's desire to com-municate became even stronger because He sent "The Word". Jesus Christ is the message of God incarnate. Everything that God wanted to say to mankind He was able to say in one Word. That Word is "Jesus". Yet, in our limited vocabulary we could never describe the glory of Christ in His fullness. It would take volumes upon volumes to give a full and accurate description of Him.

Jesus is the expression of God's thoughts toward man. In Jesus we see the attitude of God toward mankind perfectly ex-pressed. What was God trying to say when He gave His Son? Once again, volumes could not hold all of the information that God was trying to communicate to us though His Son, but if I were to condense it into one phrase I believe God would be saying "I Love You". We can see the intricate details of God's message through the life of Christ. Every miracle that Jesus performed was a message. When He healed the lame man at Bethesda He was saying "I care about those who cannot help themselves". When He fed the 5,000 He was saying many things, but we know one of them was "I care about your physical needs and will provide for you". When He came walking on the troubled sea towards the disciples He was saying "I will be with you in your trouble". The list is endless. What about the cross? What more could God do to express His love to us? God has spoken and still speaks through His Son, the Lord Jesus Christ.

III. God Speaks Through The SCRIPTURES (*The Commandments*)

God desired to speak to man so He ordained that He would write a letter. For those who are too ignorant to see His hand in creation. He desired to speak to us who just didn't seem to get the picture. God gave a Bible To those who never laid their eyes upon His Son and bowed at Jesus' feet.

God's message comes to us crystal clear through the words on the printed page. There is no guessing about His character. There is no guessing about His requirements. Everything you ever wanted to know about life or God can be found in the Holy Bible. It is a precious book and we should cherish it. It contains the Word and Words of God. Sometimes we take our Bibles for granted. Sometimes we carelessly toss them on our tables or we leave them on the dashboard of our cars to be damaged by the sun. We use them for cup holders or centerpieces on the coffee tables. Do you remember the outrage that was raised over the allegation that a Koran was flushed down the toilet by one of our American soldiers? The Muslims have laws that protect their 'holy book'. If it is touched wrong or set in the wrong place they have laws to punish the perpetrators. I believe this is extreme, but it teaches a reverence for their book. It teaches their people that the Koran is different from every other book.

Our precious Holy Bible is no ordinary book. I pray that we would have a greater reverence for it. We would not even live without the Bible **(He upholds "all things by The WORD of His power" Heb. 1:3)**. We would have no reason to come to church. We would have no faith. The Bible is the foundation of all of our beliefs. We should cherish this book more than anything on this earth – more than freedom itself.

Chapter 3
The Beginnings of the Holy Bible

T he purpose of these studies is to create within our hearts a greater reverence for The Holy Bible which we are privileged to own and use. We should cherish our Bibles more than any other object that we own. It is a priceless treasure. We should **"buy the truth and sell it not" (Prov. 23:23).**

First of all I want to look at a brief history of the English Bible as we know it. As many of you are aware, the original writings of the Bible were not written in English (there was no such thing as the English language back then), therefore, we must ask the question: How did it come to be that the Bible came to us in English? As we consider the making of the English Bible I would also like to make you aware that there is only ONE translation of the English Bible at this moment that can actually be considered to be God's Holy Word. There are many English translations today, but there is only ONE that contains the complete authority of God's Word as He intended for us to have it. It is the King James Bible.

How did we get the Bible? Where did it come from? What events took place in order to bring the Bible to us as we know it, as a book written on printed pages, bound in boards or in leather? It was not always the case. The Word of God was not so easily accessible in the days of old, but now we have it readily available to us. Let us begin with **II Timothy 3:15-17** as a text: "**And that from a child thou hast known the holy scriptures, which are able to make thee wise unto salvation through faith which is in Christ Jesus.** All scripture is given by inspiration of God, and is profitable for doctrine, for reproof, for correction, for instruction in righteousness: That the man of God maybe perfect, throughly furnished unto all good works."

Notice that in **v.15** it says "**Holy Scripture**". This will remind us that not all scripture is holy. This helps to clarify that we are not talking about an ordinary book. Neither are we talking about a book from some other religion such as Islam, Buddhism, or even New Age Christianity (Charismaticism). The King James Bible is no ordinary book - it is a Holy Book. It is a sanctified book not to be compared to any other. It is a living book (**Heb. 4:12 "For the Word of God is quick**" - the Greek definition of "quick" means "alive"). In it is embodied the very Person of Christ. You cannot separate the Living Word from the Written Word. If you read it, believe, and act upon its contents, it will produce a holy life within you.

Next, notice that **v.16** says "**all Scripture is given by inspiration of God**". First, we must ask "what scriptures"? The Scriptures that Paul is referring to here are the written manuscripts of the Hebrew Testament called the "Torah". It is what we would call the Old Testament. Paul was referring to the Old Testament. I find it interesting to note that when David wrote with such love and zeal in his Psalms about God's Word he didn't even have the entire Old Testament. He only had the Pentateuch. These books contain more law than anything else, yet David was so blessed by them. They meant more than life to him. People tend to think that the Old Testament is outdated and unusable. Ignorant and carnal believers do not consult the Old Testament because they are told it is no longer applicable in our day. Those believers who choose to omit the Old Testament or try to weaken its value by comparing it with the New Testament do themselves a great disservice. They limit themselves and will be unfulfilled and incomplete in their relationship with the Lord. Our text says "**ALL Scripture.**" **Proverbs 30:5** says "**Every Word of God is pure**". Jesus Himself, who studied only the Old Testament, spoke of its value and He deemed it necessary for spiritual life **(Matt. 4:4; Lk. 4:4)**. This is why it is beneficial to have a yearly Bible reading program. You do not merely focus upon those portions that you like, you digest every Word. Every one of His words are necessary for life. I pray that we would realize that.

The phrase in **v.16 "is given by inspiration of God"** comes from a single Greek word which means "divinely breathed in". The Holy Scriptures were breathed by God. Unlike some books which are thought out or written by men **(Tit. 1:14)**, the Bible comes from God. It would be impossible for man to create such a book. In all of man's wisdom they could never concoct a more concise, yet complete, beautiful, sublime, compilation of verse. The Scriptures were breathed by God (A man would not be able to conceive a more lovely and wonderful story than that of Jesus' life. God's love in sending His son, the Son's love in leaving heaven - **Ps 139:6 "such knowledge is too wonderful for me, it is high I cannot attain unto it"**). Man's life came from the breath of God **(Gen. 2:7)**. The Church's life came from the breath of Christ **(Jn. 20:22)**. The Holy Spirit is the breath of God and He is behind every Word of the Bible. *This is when the Bible began* - when God decided to breathe in man's direction. The Word was always there, eternal, waiting for a direction in which to move - then God blew toward mankind revealing Himself to His creation.

Wind is what gives life to words. This is the difference between words and voice. A word may only be a thought within your mind, but until air from your lungs moves across your vocal chords there is no sound. So, thoughts become spoken words with the power of breath or wind. In the book of Genesis we see the Trinity conversing (speaking words) amongst themselves as they create the heaven and the earth **(Gen. 1:26; Jn. 1:1)**. At creation God speaks and there is "light". He speaks again and the upper atmospheres separate from the water. He speaks again and the waters divide themselves from the dry land, etc.... The next intelligent life form that He speaks to are the fish and the fowl **(Gen. 1:22)**, but the conversation was limited. It was obviously one-sided. And then God speaks to man **(Gen 1:28; 2:17, 18)**. The first things that He spoke to them were of duty, dominion, delight, death, and dependence. This can all be found in a study of the first three chapters of Genesis.

The next time that we hear God speaking to man is after Adam and Eve's fall into sin **(Gen. 3:8).** The Bible says they heard the voice of the LORD God walking. They HEARD a voice that they recognized at the appointed time of the day (in the cool of the day). This voice is loud. It cannot be ignored. It cannot be forgotten. It must be heard and confronted. The voice was walking. How does a voice walk? (Let me remind us that the Word of God is Jesus. He is the embodiment of God's voice). The voice was not confined. It was seeking and searching for His lost friends. The voice was pursuing them. It was moving in man's direction. They could not escape His voice.

This is what we would call revelation. God revealed Himself to mankind instead of concealing Himself. We can see inspiration and revelation. God reveals Himself through His creation. God reveals Himself through His Spirit, but He doesn't stop there. He reveals Himself through His Word. He speaks. If we were left to understand God and His ways on our own we would never come to a complete knowledge of His truth. So, the Bible is essential. Thank God that He revealed Himself through the spoken Word. This, my friends, is the beginnings of the Bible as we know it.

The process of God's revelation:

1. His Word originated in heaven **(1 Jn. 5:7)** His thoughts, ideas, and desires toward mankind originally formulated within His heart. Here we see God the Father and His Word eternally existing.
2. Next we have inspiration or God breathing. His voice proceeds from His holy habitation. We see that Voice moving outward towards man. Here we see the Holy Ghost wind bearing the message of God to the hearts of men.
3. Now we see revelation. The breath of God reaches the earth's atmosphere and it moves upon Holy men to write the words **(2 Pet. 1:21; Heb. 1:1).**
4. These men then write in human language that which God speaks to them, namely the Old Testament written in Hebrew with some Aramaic in the book of Daniel.
5. Now we have God's Word in written form in the language

of mankind.
6. Jesus comes and we have God's Word in living form (**Heb. 1:2).**
7. The New Testament is written by the Apostles and other holy men that were inspired by the Holy Ghost(**2 Pet. 3:2).** The New Testament was written in Greek.

Once again, a simplified way of looking at the process of God's Words being translated into the language of men is:
1. Inspiration
2. Revelation
3. Original Writings
4. Translation (English or other language apart from the originals)
5. Paraphrase (Which would be considered a double-translation)

This is the order of the revelation of the Bible as we know it. We shall now try to explain some of the finer details. Numerous human instruments were used to write the Old Testament - Moses, David, Solomon, Isaiah, Jeremiah, Ezekiel, etc... (Lk. 24:44 - Moses, prophets, and psalms). These are the inspired authors of the First Testament. Their writings are what comprised the Old Testament. These are the inspired Scriptures that Jesus and the Apostles speak of in their writings (**2 Pet. 3:2).** From the Old Testament we come to the New. The Apostles wrote their epistles and these, in turn, became New Testament Scripture. And it is from all of these writings together that we have derived our Precious Holy Bible. But how did it come about? How were the books passed down and how were they chosen or even known to be inspired? How did these ancient writings last so long?

31

CHAPTER 4
THE DIVINE PRESERVATION OF
THE OLD TESTAMENT

There is no doubt that there were other ancient, religious writings and such, but only ONE true writing that was breathed by God. It is believed that the first collection of writings was made by Ezra the scribe. He and many others were inspired in the collection of the Canon of Scripture. All of them were Jews. God gave this responsibility to the Jews **(Rom. 3:2 "Oracles" means "utterances")**. It was their duty or privilege to be the instrument that God used to preserve the Old Testament Hebrew texts. These manuscripts were complete long before the time that our Lord Jesus Christ came to preach. Their form of printing in order to keep the Scriptures in circulation was limited to the work of the scribes. They were human printing presses, if you will. They tediously copied the Scriptures by hand. As far as the recognized canon of the Old Testament, they eventually came to a point when there were no more books added, altered, or removed - they became recognized as the Word of God.

The original language that was used was Hebrew, but their language eventually evolved into Aramaic. This evolved Hebrew language is what the Jews spoke during the time of Christ **(Jn. 19:20)**. The written text of the Scriptures was not readily available to every individual or even families due to the meticulous task of hand copying, so scrolls were kept and used by the Levites, Scribes, and other men of God. They were faithfully read and expounded upon on the Sabbath day and sometimes daily in public meetings **(Neh. 8:8; Lk. 4:16).** God's Word was ever kept before the people.

The process that the scribes used is astounding in many respects. Here are some of the steps taken to ensure the perfection and preservation of God's Words.

1. They were written on the skins of clean animals only or on a material called Papyrus (it is the outer rind of the bulrush that grows by the river, the same that Moses' cradle was made of). Whatever material was used, it had to be prepared by a Jew.

2. The form and layout of the writing was integral to their system. It consisted of 48 columns with no less than 16 lines per column. This is important in their writing because it was written in a mathematical form. Each letter had to be perfectly formed and the letters between the spaces had to be perfect. Not just the words had meaning, but each individual letter and the spaces between the letters had some special significance to them. The scrolls were written precisely in that form for a reason. Some did not even understand the reason, but the Jews believe that when their Messiah comes He will interpret every letter and the spaces between the letters. We, who are saved, know that He did come and that He has fulfilled the law to the furthest extent. Jesus Christ is the law interpreted.

3. The ink that was used was created especially only for the purpose of writing God's Words. It was a special recipe black ink. No other could be used.

4. To begin a new scroll the scribe would place an authentic copy before him. He would read it aloud and was careful to pronounce every word correctly before he began to copy.

5. When he wrote the word "Elohim" (Hebrew word for God) he would pause to clean his pen. When he wrote the word "Jehovah" (Hebrew word for LORD) he would wash his whole body. Can you sense the respect that they had for God and His Words? Can you imagine how long it would

take to make a copy of one book, let alone, the entire Old Testament?

6. It was then checked by other committees for mistakes. If there was one mistake on a sheet then the entire sheet was condemned. If there were three mistakes, the entire manuscript was condemned and destroyed. Such meticulous care was taken to ensure it was faithfully reproduced.

7. Every word and letter was counted every time. First they would count the letters. Then they would count the words. If the numbers did not add up correctly according to their records the entire manuscript was destroyed by burning.

This process shows the meticulous care the scribes gave to translating the Scripture. This is how the Holy Scriptures were kept in circulation for many centuries. They are the inspired Scriptures that Paul speaks of. In **Matthew 5:18** Jesus said **"For verily I say unto you, Till heaven and earth pass, one jot or one title shall in no wise pass from the law, till all be fulfilled".** The word "verily" here means "truly" or "you can count on it". You can always count on everything that Jesus has spoken, but there were certain times that He would place special emphasis on a statement that He was about to make. He wished to draw His listener's attention to His words. Next, He says "Heaven and Earth". There is not a Greek word to describe the universe, so this is the phrase they would use. The phrase, when spoken together, represents all that man is aware of around him. It would include the earth and the heavens extending beyond earth. Then He says "jot" or "tittle". A jot is the smallest letter in the Hebrew alphabet. A tittle is the small stroke which distinguishes between certain letters that are similar. In other words, He could be saying "not one dot of the 'i', or one crossing of the 't' will pass from the law". Not one jot or tittle 'shall in no wise pass'. God will preserve His Word regardless of Satan's or man's attempts to destroy it. No aspect of God's Word will ever be lost or destroyed 'until all be fulfilled'. All will be fulfilled. Everything that God has spoken will come to pass. Every prophecy of the Bible will be accomplished. There is precision in the prophecies of the Bible that cannot be denied.

Details are important to God. Small things do make a difference. Can you imagine forgetting to put the chocolate chips into chocolate chip cookies? That one necessary ingredient, if it were missing, would ruin the entire recipe. What about a mis-dialed digit in a phone number? One digit out of place will connect you to someone else. Now, when applied to the trans-lation of God's Word we see the importance of small things. Jesus mentioned the jot. The Greek word for "jot" is "iota". It means an infinitesimal amount. It means 'the tiniest piece'. The loss of a jot may not even seem important, but it could ac-tually alter the truth of God's Word.

Jesus mentioned the "tittle". It is similar to the finishing stroke that transforms an Arabic "r" to an Arabic "n". If a writer does not carefully attend to the details which distinguish an "r" from an "n" the word "bird" could easily become the word "bind". The bird looses its freedom. Those who are not diligent in obeying Christ's commands will not experience complete freedom. The more that you omit from God's Word, the more freedom you lose. Some folks think they gain free-dom by omitting words or duties found in God's Word, but actually the opposite takes place. This is also why much of the church-world today does not possess the fullness of God's power. It is because their false versions of the Bible have been minutely altered. They have removed ingredients that are es-sential to make God's Word complete and because of this their experience in incomplete.

CHAPTER 5
THE DIVINE PRESERVATION OF
THE NEW TESTAMENT

We have discussed the preservation of the Hebrew Old Testament. Now, let's talk about the New Testament. How did the New Testament books come to be accepted as inspired?

Just as the Old Testament has it's origin in God **(Gen 1:1; Jn. 1:1)**, so the New Testament has it's origin in Jesus Christ **(Matt. 1:1)**. The birth, death, burial, and resurrection of Jesus Christ necessitated the writing of the New Testament. He was the fulfiller or completer of the Old Testament **(Matt. 5:17)** and He was the originator of the New Testament. This reminds me of a verse found in *Hebrews 12:2* **"Looking unto Jesus *the Author and Finisher* of our faith ...."** Jesus is the author. He has written a library of books and compiled them into 2 volumes, completely bound into one book - The Bible. By the way, He has finished His work. There has been nothing added to it, nor taken away.

Jesus is the Author of the New Testament **(Matt. 26:28; Mk. 14:24; Lk. 22:20)**. A testament is merely a contract between two parties. In the Old Testament economy sacrificial blood was always a part of the confirmation of a religious, legal agreement. It was the signature on the dotted line, so to speak. The death of the sacrifice was symbolically used to show the solemnity of the agreement. If one of the parties were to break their oath they would, in turn, be subject to the same death. The Old Testament finds its significance and interpreter in Christ **(2 Cor. 3:14)**. The New Testament is a better testament because it is sealed in Christ's blood **(Heb. 7:22; 9:15)**.

The New Testament begins because of Christ. That is why the first books of the New Testament that we are introduced to are the Gospels. These 4 men wrote to share the "good news" of Christ's life. When Jesus had completed His earthly ministry He left His disciples with a charge - **"Go ye into all the world and preach the Gospel to every creature"** (Mk. 16:15, which, by the way, is omitted or disputed in the newer versions). In **Mattew 28:19** Jesus commands them to "teach all nations", specifically "teaching" them to observe all of His commands. Consider this charge for a moment. It would be impossible for these few men to preach everywhere. In order to teach all nations to observe the commands of Christ it seems that there would need to be writing. There would also need to be translations of that writing into various languages.

Luke wrote the largest QUANTITY of the New Testament. He begins his writing in a historical fashion in order to explain to his friend, Theophilus, the Gospel of Jesus Christ **(Lk. 1:1-4)**. He later sends another book to his friend to explain the beginnings of God's church. I am not certain if Luke was aware of his instrumentality, but it seems he had some awareness that he was being used by God because he said that he had "perfect understanding" (Lk. 1:3).

Next, we could examine the writings of Paul the Apostle. He was writing to fulfill Christ's command. He was teaching the churches the commands of Christ. So, we see that he sent letters at different times to various churches. Before this time most of these teachings were passed on by word of mouth, but these men began to write. I believe that the churches considered these epistles to be sacred. When they gathered for worship they would read them. Was Paul cognizant of his instrumentality? I believe that he may have been **(I Cor. 7:10; 2 Thess. 3:6)**. These were the first Christian writings of the churches. Peter wrote and spoke of the writings of the Apostles **(2 Pet. 3:2, 15)**. John the Beloved was the last writer of the New Testament time period. His gospel, being written much later than the others was able to include information that the others left out. He wrote from a different perspective. The main thrust of his Gospel is to defend the divinity of Jesus Christ. It is amazing that shortly after Christ's ascension the heretic's had already begun to attack His character. They were false teachers, weaseling their way into the church, who taught that Jesus was just a man. They taught that He was not of a divine, holy nature. John wrote his Gospel to equip the church against these false teachers. Today it is no different. Apostates, heretics, and false teachers are trying to destroy the character of Christ. They do it by attacking His Word. The attack on the Scriptures began early on and has not ended to this day! Corrupted versions and apocryphal books were begun early on in church history.

Satan has ever been active trying to destroy the Word of God. Satan's purpose from the beginning has been to destroy man's confidence in the Word of God **(Gen. 3:1).** He tries to bring a question into the mind of Eve concerning the Word of God. He does not come boldly with a completely false statement like: "God said you can eat what you want". He brings a question. He does not tell Eve to murder, steal, or commit adultery. He did not even tempt Eve to disbelieve in the existence of God. He attacks God's Word. This is the undermining work of Satan to this very day. Today the temptation for Christians does not come so boldly as to completely disregard God's entire Word, only certain parts of it. The temptation for the Church is to use a Bible that is more modem. Remember, that the Word of God is our foundation, and **"if the foundations be destroyed, what can the righteous do?"** (Ps. 11:3). I find it interesting that Satan convinced Eve she would become wise if she ate of this tree. It seemed as if God was keeping something good away from her. Today, these new versions claim to be wiser, better, and more improved than the Old King James Version. They try to make it sound like the King James Bible is outdated and no longer useful in our day.

Jesus exposed the nature of Satan in one of His parables. He said **"The thief comes to steal, kill, and destroy"** (Jn. 10:10). Satan's supreme objective is to overthrow or destroy God, but since that is impossible he has taken to stealing. He is a thief. He destroys things by stealing. One of the things that he steals is the Word of God. He steals from the Word of God and thereby is able to destroy God's church. Another parable of Christ's shows the thief in action. He takes away The Word from the hearts of the hearers **(Mk. 4:4, 15)**. These newer versions omit numerous passages of Scripture. God's Words are removed or taken away.

Our image of God is perceived through the Word of God. We know God by knowing His Word. *Hebrews 1:3* says that Jesus is the "express image" of the Father. Jesus is the Word. Therefore the Bible will give us a correct perception or image of God. Let me say, a PROPER Bible will give us a proper image of God. There are many different versions today that conflict with the King James Version. So, we must ask which one is right? Perverted versions will pervert the image of God. Therefore, man will worship a false God **("you worship you know not what" Jn. 4:22)**. I hate to say it, but Satan has been successful at his job. But let me also say that God has been successful at His. He said **"heaven and earth shall pass away, but MY WORDS shall not pass away" (Matt 24:35)**.

God has preserved His Word and will continue to preserve it **(Ps 12:6, 7)**. In looking at the Old Testament we learned how the Jews were the custodians of the Scripture. When we come to the NT we see that the Church takes up the torch and carries it to this day. Since the time of the apostles, the True Church has been the custodian of the Scriptures. This is why it is so important to live holy. It is imperative that we are a part of A HOLY CHURCH. In order to be a channel that God can use to keep His true Word preserved we must live holy lives because His Word is channeled through holy people **(I Pet.1:20, 21)**. This is why the True Church has constantly been persecuted, criticized, and attacked, because Satan's ultimate goal is to destroy God's Word. But, we wait for that day when The Word of God, Jesus Christ, will defeat Satan with just the Word's of His mouth (Rev. 1:16; 2:26; 2:15; 19:21).

CHAPTER 6
A HISTORICAL TIMELINE OF OUR
ENGLISH BIBLE

We will now look at various aspects of church history that will show us how the Scriptures have been preserved and how they came to be written in the English language. **Read:** *Psalm 12:6, 7; Matthew 24:35*

A.D 70-170 Was the period of circulation of the separate New Testament writings among the churches and their gradual collection into One Book - The New Testament Canon. During this period the "early church fathers" helped to authenticate what was inspired and what was not. Such men such as: Clement of Rome, Polycarp, Papias, Justin Martyr, Ignatius. Keep in mind, that some of these men sat directly under the Apostles of Christ. It was during this time, as well, that certain manuscripts began to be corrupted. These became the foundation for the manuscripts that the Roman Catholic Church would later promote.

A.D. 170-303 Early church fathers were still referring to the correct texts to use. Men such as: Iranaeus, Clement, Tertullian, Cyprian, and Origen. Lord Hailes of Scotland, who made an exhaustive study of the "Church Fathers" writings, being an authority said that if all copies of our present day New Testament should be destroyed, a New Testament could be reproduced completely with the exception of twelve verses, from these writings of the early Fathers. They believed the New Testament books were inspired and proof of that is that they quoted them as inspired. What were some of the guidelines that these men used to authenticate the inspiration of the New Testament writings?

The criteria for New Testament Canonicity was as follows:

1. Apostolicity Every book of the New Testament must either be written by an apostle or someone closely associated with an apostle.

2. Reception by the Churches The books must be universally received by the local churches as authentic at the time of their writing.

3. Consistency They must be consistent with the doctrine that the Church already possessed—namely, the Old Testament and Apostolic teaching.

4. Inspiration Each book must give evidence, internally and externally, of being divinely inspired. The spiritual gift of discernment was used to determine canonicity **(I Cor. 12:10)**.

5. Recognition Each must be recognized as canonical in the catalogues of the Church Fathers and must be used by those who had the gift of pastor-teacher.

6. Internal To be canonical, each book must contain exhortation to public exegesis of the Word **(i.e., Col. 4:16; I Thess. 5:27; I Tim. 4:13; Rev. 1:3; 2:7, 11, 17, 29; 3:6, 13; also Peter's famous statement at the end of his second epistle. Although Paul had thoroughly braced Peter in Galatians 2:6-14, Peter places Paul's writings on a par with the Old Testament Scriptures in II Peter 3:15-16).** {Taken from R. B. Theime's Canonicity}

Once again, God uses holy vessels to preserve His words. "It has been truly said that the Bible is not an authorized collection of books, but a collection of authorized books."-Frank Gaebelien. In other words, just because man has stamped their seal of approval upon them did not make them authentic. They were already authentic and inspired and it was God that gave godly men the wisdom to discern the difference between the false and the true. God was the One that supervised the process of creating the Canon and without His hand in it; we would all have been deceived. As Martin Luther wisely observed, "There is for us of a latter day another test of Canonicity". According to his belief, those books are canonical which contain Christ and which thus bear witness to the spirit of him who reads it.

A.D. 303-379 It was during this period that the Emperor of Rome, Diocletian, began his persecution the Churches. Diocletian had set out to annihilate the Christians and their Holy Book. This was a troubled time for the Christian Church. It was also during this period, and in the years shortly thereafter, that the great church councils were held. They resulted in the formal ratification of the Canon, which by then had been in existence for several hundred years. From this point the New Testament was set in stone. The Old Testament Canon had already been recognized by the Jews and now the New Testament was completed. In 397 the Senate of Carthage declared the 27 books of the New Testament and the 39 books of the Old Testament to be accepted as inspired Scripture. The apocrypha was included, but there was a footnote attached that declared it to be only for the use of instruction and it was not considered to be inspired. The question of canonicity never came up again until the rise of liberalism in the nineteenth century, which led to our twentieth century modernism – textual criticism.

A.D. 382 Jerome, an outstanding scholar of his day, translated the Greek New Testament into Latin. This was called the "Vulgate".

A.D. 400 By this time the Bible had been translated into 500 different languages. The church at Rome stopped the uses of any language except for Latin. Only one language was allowed for education and instruction. Therefore the ignorant or average person would not be able to read the Scriptures. They had to rely upon the priests to read them and expound them. The catholic priests read from corrupted versions and expounded deceptions to the people. But there was always a remnant. From this point in history for approximately 1000 years was the period termed the "dark" or "middle ages". The Roman church was in power. The Pope had the final say as to what was from God. During this time period there were gleams of light proceeding still from God's inspired Scriptures.

A.D. 680 Caedmon sang the Scriptures in the language of the common people, which was English.

A.D. 640-709 Aldhelm translated the psalms into Anglo-Saxon.

A.D. 647-735 Bede, the most learned man and the most famous writer of Anglo-Saxon times, was a believer. He was convinced that the people needed a translation of the Gospel. He translated the Gospel of John.

A.D. 871-901 Alfred the Great, King of England is famous for many accomplishments, but his most notable deed for the Church was giving his subjects a translation of the Bible that they could understand.

A.D. 1330-1384 A lot of commotion began to stir about this time. The dark ages were about to come to an end because a great light arose to shine forth the truth of the Gospel and the Word of God. His name was John Wycliffe. John Wycliffe was a born-again priest who began to see the inaccuracies of the Vulgate. Not only had the Apocrypha found its way into the Vulgate, but also many interpretations of Hebrew expositors had been incorporated into the text. Wycliffe decided it was necessary for him to come up with a new translation. He was the most powerful preacher of his day. He was a respected teacher and President of Oxford College in England. It was here; in his preaching and teaching that he began to refute Catholic doctrines. From his own studies he came to the conclusion that the Bible and Christ alone were man's supreme authority - not the Pope or the Church of Rome. In order to break the darkness that had overshadowed England for almost six centuries Wycliffe felt that the only way to help the people was to get the Bible to them in their language. He translated the Latin Vulgate into English. Without a printing press it would take ten months to make a copy by hand. In order to spread the Gospel, Wycliffe commissioned men that came to be termed as "lollards". These disciples would travel everywhere with a copy of Wycliffe's translation and share the Word with people. These lollards received much persecution from the church and some were martyred. The pope was contriving a way to stop Wycliffe. He labeled him a heretic and tried to bring about his trial and death.

A.D. 1384-1539 Even years after Wycliffe's death, the Bible was persecuted by the church because it was in such great demand. People would pay large sums of money for just one leaf of the Scriptures; sometimes a load of hay was given just to be able to read a portion for one hour. In 1408 the archbishop of York gathered the church hierarchy together to discredit Wycliffe's Bible. They made a decree that it was unlawful to translate the Bible into English. It was an authorized prohibition of the English Scriptures. In 1416 John Hus, a disciple of Wycliffe and a promoter of his teachings, was tried and burnt at the stake. Actual manuscripts that his students had copied were used for the kindling. John Hus prophesied that in 100 years someone would come, who they would not be able to stop. That man was Martin Luther (for the purposes of our study of the English Bible we will not focus upon his life). In 1428, 44 years after Wycliffe's death, the church's hatred for him and his Bible still smoldered. Pope Martin had his bones dug up, burned, and thrown into the River Swift. They thought they had taken care of God's Word, but their plan was about to backfire. Around 1455 the first printing press was used. With the Gutenberg Press, the Word of God could be printed and distributed in unlimited numbers.

It was during this period that a man named William Tyndale rose to prominence. But, before we discuss his life we will look briefly at a few other great men who where used to influence him. In 1490 Lineacre studied the Greek language in Greece. He was disturbed to find that the Latin Bible he had known all this time did not line up correctly. He said "either this is not the Bible, or we are not Christians." He saw that the Latin text was corrupt from the meaning that God had intended. Also, around this time was a man named John Colet. He visited a preacher named Savonarola. Savonarola, a born-again priest who seemed to be isolated from the rest of the world, preached the Word of God in the language of the people. There was great revival under his pastorate. The building could not hold the crowds that would flock to hear him preach. John Colet was deeply affected by this. He returned to Oxford University in London and preached only the Greek text in English, without exposition. Within one month of this "new" service, the chapel was packed. He did the same at St. Paul's Cathedral. Within six months there were 15-20,000 people trying to get in for one service to be able to hear the Scriptures read in their own English language.

Erasmus, one of the most brilliant men who ever lived, took up the burden to translate the Bible into English. Many discouraged him from doing it. In 1514 he assembled a Greek text for the printing press. In the preface of his new work he wrote "I vehemently dissent from those who are unwilling that the Sacred Scriptures, translated into the common tongue, should be read by private persons ... I would wish even all women to read the Gospel and Epistles of St. Paul, and I wish that they were translated into all languages of all Christian people. I wish that the husbandman may sing parts of them at his plow, that the weaver may warble them at his shuttle, that the traveler may with their narratives beguile the weariness of the way". Erasmus' translation became the foundation for Luther's translation and Tyndale's translation about 9 years later.

William Tyndale, born in 1494, died in 1539. He died in exile and in poverty. An outlaw, hunted for 11 years by kings and by the Roman church. His background is astounding. He enrolled at Oxford at about 12 years of age and received his masters' degree at age 23. He spoke eight different languages fluently. He founded the "White Horse Society". As he received his education at Oxford he sat under Erasmus. It was shortly after he left Cambridge, to become the tutor-chaplain of the Walsh Estate that he began to notice the corruption of the leaders of the Catholic Church. It was then that he felt his life's work to be that of bringing the Bible to the people in theft own language.

A few years after Erasmus had made his translation in 1517, five men and two women were burned at the stake - Their crime: Teaching the Lord's Prayer to their children in English. During this time there was widespread persecution. Tyndale came under suspicion for his views on the Authority of Scripture and the interpretation of the Bible. In a heated discussion with a certain Bishop in a local parlor the Bishop said that he revered the Pope's authority over Scripture (and why not - the

Pope is God's chosen representative of "the church" - God supposedly speaks through him). Tyndale got 'beside himself and said "I defy the Pope and all his laws, and if God would spare my life these many years, I will make it possible that the boy who drives the plough will be able to know as much Scripture as you do".

After this statement he was warned by the most powerful Bishop in Bristol that if he continued to teach in English the things of God he would suffer the consequences. In 1524, with the assistance of the secret society, he fled to Germany to meet with Luther. Then he went to Cologne to print the New Testament in English for the first time. Bounty hunters had been commissioned to seek him and were hot on his trail. They were actually going to nab him at Cologne because they had received intelligence that he was heading there to print the Bibles. Tyndale also was tipped about the danger of the bounty hunters and was able to reach the press, snatch what remaining leaves were on print only minutes before his captors arrived. He immediately fled upriver in a raft to Worms. Here he was able to find a short recluse from those that were hunting his life and he was able to have 6000 copies of his New Testament printed, loaded onto ships hidden in other merchandise, and shipped to England.

In October of 1526, Bishop Tunstall denounced Tyndale's Bible in English and copies were publicly burned. A royal decree by King Henry VIII stated, "We, with deliberate advice of the most reverend father (Pope), have determined the said and untrue translations to be burned, with sharp correction and punishment against the keepers and readers of the same." Their plan to bring fear upon the people backfired and only created more interest in "The Forbidden Book". The bishop declared that he would give large sums of money for as many copies as he could gather with the intent to destroy them. It is somewhat sad, yet humorous that at this time an unfortunate Lollard was arrested and brought to trial in London. During his hearing, the judge asked him if he knew who was helping William Tyndale print so many Bibles. He replied "the Bishop of London is doing more to help than anyone else, for the money paid for the Bibles that are burned is used to print and circulate fresh copies." Tyndale was using the money to improve his copies and increase his printing. Enraged by William Tyndale's success, Henry VIII employed a treacherous spy named Phillips to lure Mr. William Tyndale from the protection of his home in Antwerp. Fooled by an invitation to dinner, Mr. Tyndale was captured and imprisoned in the castle of Vilvorde.

William Tyndale was publicly accused of the following crimes during his trial.

1. He had maintained that faith alone justifies.
2. He maintained that to believe in the forgiveness of sins and to embrace the mercy offered by the Gospel was enough for salvation.
3. He maintained that human traditions cannot bind the conscience.
4. He denied that there is a purgatory
5. He affirmed that neither the Virgin Mary nor the saints pray for us.

Mr. Tyndale was taken out of prison on October 6, 1536. His last words were, "Lord, open the king of England's eyes". He was then strangled by the court executioner and burned at the stake. Five years later, a Bible that had been published by William Tyndale under the fictitious name of Thomas Matthew was presented to Henry VIII. After reading portions of it, he ordered that every church in his kingdom should receive a copy. There were 20,000 copies printed. This was called "The Great Bible". William Tyndale's prayer had been answered. {taken from a Wisdom Worksheet by Bill Gothard}

A.D. 1550 Robert Stevens separated the type into verses.

A.D. 1553 It was during this time that the rift between Protestants and Catholics began to widen. I do not fully understand all of the historical intricacies at this point, but during this time under the reign of Queen Mary the Christians suffered greatly. She wished to burn every protestant that would not submit to the church in Rome. John Rogers, who printed the first 'legal' English Bible, was burned first because he was closest to Tyndale. Miles Coverdale, who printed the first English version of Luther's Bible, was able to escape to Geneva, Switzerland. Many Christians fled from England to Geneva. Those who did not flee were herded like cattle and burned in large groups. It would often take hours for a person to die depending on how the wind was blowing. During this time over 300 leading prot-estant scholars and preachers would be burned under Mary's four year reign. A lot of background information from this era can be gleaned from Foxe's Book of Martyrs. These men haz-arded their lives for the Gospel's sake (Acts 15:26; 20:24).

A.D. 1560 While in Geneva, John Knox and Miles Coverdale decided to print Tyndale's Bible with marginal notes. This was called the Geneva Bible. It was the standard for 200 yrs. It was the Bible of the pilgrims and puritans.

A.D. 1560-1610 During this period in 1582 the Jesuit Bible was printed in English at Rheims, France. They dominated 287 col-leges and universities throughout Europe. They were trying to counteract the spread of Protestantism. In 1604 the puritans appealed to King James about the translation of a new Bible into English. Immediately the Bishop of London and others opposed such an idea, but after much debate the King was per-suaded that a new translation was necessary. Although King James sided with the puritans he still had certain requirements that needed to be met before they could begin their work. The most significant requirement was that he would be able to ap-point the translators.

A.D. 1611 From this came what is now known as the Author-ized King James Bible. Through the years there were slight grammatical corrections and "polishings". The version we cur-rently use was finalized around 1769.

CHAPTER 7
WHICH VERSION IS THE WORD OF GOD?

e have learned the most important thing that makes the Bible so precious is because it is The Word of God. But, in our day we run into some difficulties because there are so many different versions. However, Bible scholars claim that these various versions are *all* "the word of God". They also claim that they have been made easier to understand for English speaking people. They say they have been simplified and modernized in order to be relevant to the current generation. This seems to be a noble undertaking on the part of the translators. They see the gaping chasm that spans between the church and the world and they realize that only the Word of God can help this sinful world, so they set out with a desire to help the heathen of America by creating a "New" and "Improved" Bible with the hopes that God would be better understood.

There are many problems that arise out of this theory. There are Bibles for different age groups or genders. There are Bibles for different races, skin colors, and sexual orientation. One problem that arises from this is that the Bible version a person chooses becomes a matter of personal preference. "I choose that Bible" or "This Bible fits me better" or "This Bible is more of my style". This is a big problem because it robs God of His holiness. Yes, I understand that the Apostle Paul said "...I am made all things to all men, that I might by all means save some" (I Cor. :22). Yes, Paul may have become all things to all men, but he took something with him that stayed the same. Paul may change, but The Word of God does not change. Yes, Jesus came to the sinners, He was a friend of sinners, He ate with sinners, but the Bible also says that He was separate from sinners (Heb. 7:26). He was with them physically, but spiritually, mentally, and morally He was high above them – separate from them. If we change our Bibles for every group or sect, then we rob God of His distinctive separateness. These worldly sinners need to be the ones to COME to THE UNCHANGING WORD OF GOD. The danger with the Bible in our day is that we would simplify it for those around us. People say they cannot understand it. They say that its Words are archaic – it is part of the Bronze Age. While it may be true that they don't understand some of the language, do we corrupt our Bibles for their benefit? EDUCATION HAS FAILED! The Bible says to "APPLY thine heart to understanding" (Prov. 2:2). My challenge to those who do not understand the King James Bible is to go to your knees in earnest prayer until the Holy Ghost enlightens your mind and becomes your Teacher. He will never fail!

However, this is not the main problem that these new versions create. They all claim to be God's Word made in such a way to be more easily understood. We all would wish that people could understand God better, but here's the main issue. Most of these new versions and translations all agree with each other except for one – The King James Version. Every version that has deviated from the Textus Receptus unites with each other to stand in opposition to the King James Bible. Just about every modern translation, with the small exception of a few, is taken from corrupted manuscripts and defies the Truths found in the King James Bible. The sad fact is that the average person does not take the time to do an in-depth comparison, so they are swept into this notion that these newer versions are actually easier to understand. They sincerely believe that they have God's Word when they have an English translation other than the King James Bible. They may be similar, but they are not the same. They are counterfeits. Satan has been in the business of trying to counterfeit God's Words and works since the beginning. There are masters of manipulation out there that can make fake money look real. There are con-artists that can create identical copies of artwork or other objects of value. To the untrained eye they are the same, but a specialist can see the difference. On the same token, Pharaoh's magicians were able to produce extraordinary things. How did they do the same things Moses did? Moses operated through the power of God, the magicians through the power of Satan. Satan counterfeits God's works (**Ex. 7:11**). We see this is evident in today's charismatic church where they have allowed Jezebel's and Balaam's doctrines to corrupt the truth.

Not only does Satan counterfeit God's works, he also counterfeits God's Words. Paul said in *Galatians 1:6-12:*

"**I marvel that ye are so soon removed from him that called you into the grace of Christ unto another gospel: Which is not another; but there be some that trouble you, and would pervert the gospel of Christ. But though we, or an angel from heaven, preach any other gospel unto you than that which we have preached unto you, let him be accursed. As we said before, so say I now again, If any man preach any other gospel unto you that that ye have received, let him be accursed. For do I now persuade men, or God? Or do I seek to please men? For if I yet pleased men, I should not be the servant of Christ. But I certify you, brethren, that the gospel which was preached of me is not after man. For I neither received it of man, neither was I taught it, but by the revelation of Jesus Christ.**"

There is "another" gospel that Satan preaches. We must be able to distinguish between what is true and which one is the counterfeit. When you bring these modern versions under scrutiny you will find that there are many words omitted and there are doctrinal and theological contradictions. Strangely enough, there is one thing that all of these Bible versions have in common and that is they all agree with one another, but they all align themselves to disagree with the King James Bible. So, if these new "improved" versions claim to be God's Word and the King James Bible makes the same claim only ONE of them is making a correct claim. Which one is right? Which Bible is actually The Word of God? Wouldn't you agree that it is vitally important to be sure that you know you have the True Word of God? If the Bible is our foundation for everything that we believe as Christians, it is imperative that we have God's Words as He intended for us to have them. *Psalm 11:13* says: **"If the foundations be destroyed, what can the righteous do?"**

Which Bible version *IS* the *REAL* Word of God? In doing this study and taking the time to examine the different versions it caused me to realize the confusion in this matter of "versions". People are faced with countless choices. Which one do I choose as my Bible? The fact that there are so many versions generates confusion – God is not the author of confusion. We, who believe in the King James Bible as the only authoritative English rendition of God's Holy Word, are blamed for being the cause of the 'confusion problem'. At least, that's what the people say who oppose the King James Bible. We believe in a standard.

We believe in an Authorized Version – one that has been authorized by the Holy Ghost. We believe in its exclusiveness and to this date there has not been another version available to rival its textual accuracy and readability, therefore we cause confusion because we claim that it is superior to every other version. Yet even if there were no King James Bible there is confusion because there are so many versions which compete for your money. There is also the confusion that is created within a church body. If the churches do not set a standard then which Bible is predominately used? It creates confusion when the preacher reads from a certain version and others in the congregation read from another. It creates confusion in families. When Grandma and Grandpa swore by the King James Bible's precious truth, and now their grandchildren do not see eye – to –eye with their grandparent's beliefs. So, we see there is a need for clarification. What is the difference between these many versions and the King James Bible? These other "versions" are not really versions, but rather "perversions" of God's precious Word, and it is my prayer that through this study you will recognize that there is only One True version of the Word of God in the English language – the King James Bible.

CHAPTER 8

THIS CHAPTER IS CONDENSED, WITH COMMENTS BY THE AUTHOR, FROM DR. D. A. WAITE'S BOOK ENTITLED "DEFENDING THE KING JAMES BIBLE" WITH PERMISSION.

Speaking of foundations, we will now begin to look at some foundational principles that will show us why the King James Bible is superior to all other English translations. There are 4 categories that will help us to build a solid argument by which to convince the gainsayers of our day:

1. Texts
2. Translators
3. Technique
4. Theology

TEXTS

If God has been gracious enough to speak to mankind and we realize that He originally spoke only in Hebrew, Aramaic, and Greek, then we must be certain that our English translation contains the entirety of God's Words. I believe that our King James Bible accurately preserves the proper Hebrew and Greek words in the English language and accurately translates those divinely preserved Words. God has promised to preserve His Word **(Ps. 12:6, 7)** and we are blessed to be able to have it in our English language.

In order to have a proper English translation we must first have the proper Hebrew and Greek manuscripts. This is the first reason why I believe that the King James Bible is God's preserved Words in English – because it was translated from superior manuscripts. The Old Testament Hebrew text that is used as the foundation for our King James Bible is called the "Traditional Masoretic Hebrew Old Testament Text". It was handed down throughout many generations by a sect of traditional Jews called the "Masoretes". The modern versions (at this point we will define 'modern' by beginning with the Revised Version of 1881 to the present) do not use the Masoretic text. For instance, the New American Standard Version uses Kittel's Biblia Hebraica along with other sources. When you compare this with the King James Bible there are approximately. 25,000 changes – some of these are major, some minor, but we must be reminded of our Lord's statement that not ONE jot or tittle would not pass from the law. We can see another case in point with the New International Version which has used up to 15 different sources to complete their Old Testament. By using 15 different sources they are able to sound "scholarly" by showing how they have compared every source available to come up with the "most accurate" and "complete" version available. The problem is that they do not inform you when they may use a different source – it is left up to their own discretion. Although they use the Masoretic Text in some areas they disregard it in others. If you are not certain which original text was used for your translation then you cannot be certain that you have God's True Words.

The original text that we use to translate a Bible is like the foundation that we use to build a house. If the foundation is faulty then the house will not stand. Although an original text may be "old" or "authentic" you must find the source for that manuscript. If the source is questionable then your manuscript is faulty and will not provide a proper foundation for your translation. The problem with the modern versions is that they have completely disregarded the most proven and reliable source which has been accepted by the Jews for centuries and have substituted it with what they "feel" is better. Some editors of these false Bibles have admitted that sometimes they have no reason to deviate from the Masoretic text, but they do because they feel that it would "read better". They base their deviation from the true text upon conjecture. In other words, there is no reason for their departure from the Masoretic text. My question is "What if they made a wrong guess?" Would you like your eternal soul to be held in the hands of someone who merely guesses that they have made a proper translation? It is evident, through comparative study that the King James translators did not deviate from the Masoretic text – they faithfully translated it right over into the English without making any "guesses".

We can trust the Masoretic text because it was accumulated by the Jews, but it was also authorized by the Lord Jesus Christ. Often we find the Lord quoting from the Old Testament. When he was in warfare with Satan He refuted the devil's temptations with The Word. He said in *Matthew 4:4* **"IT IS WRIT-TEN, man shall not live by bread alone, but by EVERY WORD that proceedeth out of the mouth of God."** Jesus had confidence in the Words of God that had been written down many years prior to His coming. He recognized them to be God's inspired and preserved Words. He quoted from the same text that underlies our King James Bible. On more than one occasion He mentioned the Law and the Prophets with the utmost confidence and respect. He had confidence that the Masoretic text had been accurately transmitted. By the way, he never refuted any text, any word, or any letter of the Old Testament. The Masoretic Old Testament text is THE firm foundation that our King James Bible is built upon.

Not only is the King James Bible superior in its Old Testament translation, but also in the New. The New Testament was translated from the Greek Textus Receptus ("Received Text"). The text used predominately in seminaries or colleges whether they be conservative or liberal is the Nestle/Aland Greek New Testament text. Most modern versions are translated from this corrupted text or others. The most notable feature about the Nestle/Aland text is that it has undergone a revision approximately every 3 years. That implies that these "educated professionals" are unsure of the accuracy of their own version. If they have made 26 editions in 81 years (1898-1979) then what about the first edition? What about the second? Were these correct? No, but many people were led to believe that they were. It took them 26 editions to perfect their deception and it's still not right! Also, before you go running out there to purchase one of these "new" and "better'" bibles why don't you stop to consider the theological beliefs of the editors? They are unbelievers and apostates who have brought in damnable heresies, such as denying the virgin birth and divinity of Christ. Would you like to read their "bible"? How could they possibly come up with a correct and unbiased translation?

It's amazing how accurate the Textus Receptus is. It hasn't had a revision in the last 381 years and every revision before that was based upon minor changes of language evolution. We can thank John Wycliffe and William Tyndale for their labors, but more importantly we can thank God that He used these men to help preserve His Words. Our King James Bible is 5/6th' to 9/10th' phrased like William Tyndale's translation. Now that's a steadfast translation! The Textus Receptus has been "received" and accepted by Godly saints of days gone by and it has been attested by undeniable evidence that it is THE superior text.

Most of the efforts to destroy credibility in the King James Bible in our day had its beginnings in 1881. Before this time there was scattered opposition to the received text, but it had its culmination in 1881, when 2 Anglican theologians began to undertake a new translation. Westcott was a bishop of the Anglican Church. Hort was a teacher at Cambridge University. They were secretly involved in questionable practices and their theology was severely corrupt. Yet they were able to deceive many scholars of their day into helping them create what they said was a "better" text. It is called "The Revised Version". Maybe you've heard of it. Remember it well, for it is from this text that the downward trend of downgrading God's Words began. You can scarcely find a Bible college or seminary these days that uses the Textus Receptus – they tend to rely upon the Revised Greek Text or upon the Nestle/Aland Greek text. We can see the culture of corruption that pervades American culture, and we can see the modern church has left the old paths for a new revelation. What is the cause of this awful decline? I believe that it is a direct result of tampering with God's Holy Word. Without Bible schools that teach their preachers right we will not have right churches. Without right churches we will not have right families and without right families we will not have a right country. Before 1960 the average layperson used the King James Version, although the scholars had been using the Revised Version for years. The deception that the New American Standard Version was better slowly trickled down to the people. You can notice a marked change in America's morality in the 60's. How were they able to convince the people to switch versions? Did they advertise that it was time to accept a corrupted version that was changed in thousands of places? No, they sold it on the basis that "The King James Version can no longer be understood". "We need something that is more up to date and current". Where did this notion come from? These so-called scholars created the problem and publishing companies benefited immensely from their endorsement of these false bibles. What I find amazing is that it was the scholars that created this notion, when simple, ordinary folks for centuries had used the King James Bible without any difficulty. Grandma and Grandpa were able understand it and live by it. The backwoods holiness preachers who had never been to college were able to comprehend it and preach it. Today people want a bible that they can understand. The sad fact is they are able to understand these corrupted versions. I believe that even this modern generation can understand the King James Bible if they truly desire to. Anyone who truly desires to lay hold on eternal life will do everything in their ability to understand God and the Bible He gave us.

Today people want a Bible that they can understand. I find it interesting to note that some of the modern versions are actually harder grammatically to understand than the King James Bible. They use larger words per syllable and more obscure words. The readability index of the King James Bible has been placed between a 6th and 10th grade reading level and many children who have not even reached these grade levels are able to understand it with the greatest of ease. One of the main reasons that people do not understand the King James Bible is because they do not TRY to understand it. They simply accept the lie that it is outdated. They accept the lie that these modern version are easier to understand. But here is the problem: When you tamper with the Words of the Bible you must remember that you are not just tampering with printed words. Jesus said **"The Words that I speak unto you, they are spirit and they are life" (Jn. 6:63).** The Words of the Bible are Life –

They are spiritual in nature. The Bible is a spiritual book which speaks to the spiritual nature of mankind. But when you remove, add, or change these words you are tampering with the spiritual nature of God's Word. You not only remove words, but you remove its ability to remove sin out of your life. When you change it, you change its ability to change your heart. A carnal man can understand a carnal, man-made bible, but remember: *1 Corinthians 2:14* **"But the NATURAL MAN receiveth NOT the things of the Spirit of God: for they are foolishness unto him: neither can he know them, because they are SPIRITUALLY DISCERNED."** There are consequences to having a wrong bible.

Westcott and Hort's Greek text is so wrong that there are at least 5,604 changes from the Textus Receptus: 1,952 are OMISSIONS (35%), 467 are ADDITIONS (8%), and 3,185 are CHANGES (57%). That means that on the average, each page of their text would have 15.4 deviations from the Textus Receptus or a total of 7% difference between the Revised Version and the King James Bible. That would be the equivalent to the amount of words in the books of 1 & 2 Peter. Just go ahead and rip 'em out! Now, the scholars make the claim that there are no doctrinal changes in these "new" bibles; they are just 'easier to understand'. Yes, they may be shorter and easier to understand, but they are also missing vital Words that the Lord wanted in there. How can they say that their version is no different? It is different to the tune of thousands of words and it is lacking in Truth. How many changes does it take before your Bible is no longer 100% God's Words? JUST ONE. You cannot truly hold one of these 'modern' versions in your hand and claim that you have God's Word. You may have small portions or parts of God's Word, but you do not have it in its fullness.

We see how important it is to have proper manuscripts for the translation of a Bible. We know that the Textus Receptus Greek New Testament text has its roots in the translations of Wycliffe and Tyndale. Where did they get their foundations? They got theirs from various church fathers who gained their texts from the apostles themselves. Where did Westcott & Hort get the foundations for their Greek New Testament? They relied upon a combination of different manuscripts, mainly those of B and Aleph. B is the Vatican manuscript and Aleph is the

Sinai manuscript. They claim that these manuscripts are older, therefore they carry more authority. On the contrary, I believe it is proof that they were unused manuscripts. They may be older, and they survived longer because they were not used. The reason why they were not used is because those in the True Church recognized them as false. If they had been used frequently they would have been like many of our worn-out Bibles. It is somewhat humorous where these manuscripts were obtained. The Aleph manuscript was found in a wastepaper basket at St. Catherine's Monastery. They were getting ready to burn it to keep warm for the winter. Dr. Tischendorf, a German critical scholar, was working on a translation of the New Testament when he found this manuscript. He paid hundreds of dollars for TRASH. The monks realized its worthlessness and were ready to burn it! But this apostate preacher retrieved it and was able to corrupt the church with its leaven. There are many other facts which we could consider in our study, but it is not my purpose to do so at this time. It is my understanding that our King James Bible is superior to the modern versions because it is based upon superior Hebrew and Greek texts. Thanks be unto God for His unspeakable gift – this good gift, our Precious Holy Bible, came from Him in Whom is no variableness neither shadow of turning and we can be assured of its unfailing accuracy.

TRANSLATORS

If the manuscripts or texts that we use to translate a Bible are like the foundation we build a house upon, then the people who do the work of translating are like the builders we hire to build our house. If you were to build a house, who would you prefer? - A company that has only been in business for 1 year or a successful company of 30 years who has a name for quality? If we had our choice we would choose the company with the most experience because they can be trusted to build us a house that will be able to stand when the strong winds blow upon it. They can be trusted to build us a house, not one upon foundations of sand, rather, one that will not topple under the severe rains that will beat upon it. The same is true for the bible version you choose to read. Have you ever considered who may have been on the editorial or translation committee? Have you ever taken the time to research the lives that they lived and their theological positions? These are important things to keep in mind when you are considering the translation you will rely upon to be your blueprint for a successful home here on earth and in heaven. The good thing is that there have been scholars who have researched this for us so we can be informed about the people behind various translations.

It is not the author's intention to spend a great deal of time on this section of our study except to bring to our attention the fact that there are many differences in the lives of the people who have been involved in different translations. In the next chapter we will discuss the attitudes and intentions behind the methods of translation, but now we shall consider the moral and educational advantage that the King James translators had over recent scholars. Virtually every man on the translation committee for the King James Bible was a believer. They were spiritual men who had a personal commitment to the Lord and His Word. They held to the basic, cardinal beliefs that we would consider necessary to be an evangelical, Bible-believing Christian. Some of them were known to be outstanding preachers and men of prayer. Does that sound like some men you could trust?

On the other hand, it is a known fact that one of the women on the translation committee for the New International Version was/is a lesbian. Many of the modern translators have no personal relationship with the Lord. In fact, they hold views that are contrary to the Scriptures such as: denying the virgin birth of Christ, denying that salvation only comes through Christ's blood, denying the necessity for a holy life, denying THE INNERANCY OF SCRIPTURE (isn't that funny??), and many more deviations from the Truth. But that's OK because they are more informed and better educated than these old-fashioned scholars. I think that you would have a hard time finding such skilled men as the King James translators. Many of them knew a number of Biblical languages so well, that they were more fluent than those who actually spoke the languages. Some were scholars with such determination that they studied for up to 16 hours a day consistently. Here are just a few names to keep in mind: Lancelot Andrews, William Bedwell, Miles Smith (wrote the preface to the King James Bible – Have you ever read it?), Henry Savile, John Bois, and others. It seems that God had prepared these men for such a time to bring about an accurate translation of His Word for the English speaking people. The moral and educational deficiencies of our modern day translators have created deficient versions which have corrupted the minds of many. The 'structures' that they have erected will not stand against 'every wind of doctrine' and neither will you or the church that chooses to rely upon these deficient versions for refuge. Thank God for the King James translators who have built for us a secure translation which has stood the test of time! By the way, King James may have had personal faults, but he was not even on the translation committee. He just authorized and commissioned the work to be undertaken.

TECHNIQUE

Any contractor who builds a house has certain methods by which he works. Hopefully he would have the right materials and he would be able to read a blueprint. I heard of a contractor who has built houses for customers by using old lumber that had been saved from a previous demolition. The wood was cracked, weathered, had nail holes and other deficiencies. Needless to say, he was sued. Have you ever seen some of the methods people use to build houses? Some may claim "We do it all", but they don't do it right. They may piece something together for you, but it is not plumb, level, or square – they build it as they go without consulting a print and the results are devastating. The method that a builder uses to build a house is like the TECHNIQUE that the translators use to create a version.

There are some outstanding characteristics found in the techniques of the King James translators that make the King James Bible superior to the modern versions. They had a superior TEAM technique. Most of the modern-day versions are translated by a few men who use others to help them smooth out the English style. But in the case of the King James Bible all 54 men involved had to be so skilled in the languages that they had to make their own translation of the books they were assigned to translate. For example, those who were in the Oxford Old Testament Group had to be able to translate seventeen books (from Isaiah to Malachi). There were eight men on this committee and each one had to make their own personal translation of these books. That is quite an undertaking, unless you are familiar with the languages involved.

There were certain rules that the translators used to help create a superbly accurate translation. For instance, as I have already mentioned, each man on the different committees had to make their own translation of the section that was assigned to them. With an average of 7 men on a committee that means it was being translated 7 different times. They would then disperse it amongst themselves to come up with the agreed translation. After the committee agreed on their portion of the translation they would then send it to the other 6 committees for review. Once that was agreed upon there would be a final analysis and correction at the end by 12 distinguished men from each of the committees. This would make a total of 14 times that the Bible from Genesis to Revelation was translated creating a translation that was perfectly complete **(Psalm 12:6)**. One of the miracles of this system is that you had a variety of great men who were each educated beyond the ordinary measure, but had to come to an agreement upon the final translation. If they did not agree on a certain reading, portion, or verse it would not pass until they were all completely satisfied that it was correct. Dr. D. A. Waite has found that such a system has not been used for modern translations. Basically, a version is promoted by one person who is considered to be a great scholar, who may put his endorsement or 'stamp of approval' upon a revision, but those on the committee do not have to individually translate the books by themselves. Many of the modern versions are not even translations – they are paraphrases. They are translations of translations. It is simply taking a version that has already been translated from the original languages and making a revision. They take an English translation and redefine the English. There is no skill involved in that – you or I could make such a version! It is a shame that God's Words are treated with such disrespect.

It would also be well to consider the motives and method behind the translators. The King James Translators used a system which we call "verbal and formal equivalence". In other words the words from the Greek or Hebrew were rendered as closely as possible into the English. They had a respect for God's Word and were more determined to allow the texts to say what they meant in a word for word fashion. The method that is used by modern translators is called "dynamic equivalence" in which they use what they "feel" would be the right word or phrase to use at a certain time. They are not as concerned with the word for word reading, but they translate according to what they "think" God is trying to say in a particular passage or verse. This is basically called "COMMENTARY" which is a dangerous form of translation because what if your "thoughts" or "feelings" about God's message is not correct? They not only deceive themselves, but countless unwary sheep are led astray.

Where did this technique of dynamic equivalence come from and what is involved in it? I believe that Satan originated this translation technique many years ago. In this technique we see the principle of SUBTRACTION. *Genesis 3:1* says **"Now the serpent was more subtil than any beast of the field which the LORD God had made. And He said unto the woman, Yea, hath God said, ye shall not eat of every tree of the garden?"** Here we see he subtracted from God's original statement. We must look back to *Genesis 2:16, 17* to see God's original statement: **"And the LORD God commanded the man, saying, Of every tree of the garden thou mayest freely eat, BUT of the tree of the knowledge of good and evil, *thou shalt not eat of it:* for in the day that thou eatest thereof thou shalt surely die."** Satan did mention part of God's statement, but he removed part of it as well. This led to Eve's fall from innocence. The modern translators also use this method by subtracting things that they feel are no longer relevant. We have no right to remove any of God's Words. He meant what He said, therefore we should do our best to preserve and keep it.

We can also see where the dynamic equivalency technique CHANGES the Word of God. Satan not only subtracted from God's Words, he also changed them. God said in *Genesis 2:17* **"...for in the day that thou eatest thereof thou shalt surely** die." We can see Satan's revision of God's Words in *Genesis 3:4* **"And the serpent said unto the woman, <u>Ye shall NOT surely die.</u>"** That one, little, three-letter word NOT changed the entire meaning of God's statement. God made it clear that the results of disobedience would be death, but Satan tries to portray God as a liar.

Not only did Satan subtract and change God's Words, but he also added to them. Satan said to Eve in *Genesis 3:5* **"For God doth know that in the day ye eat thereof, then your eyes shall be opened, and ye shall be as gods, knowing good and evil."** God never made or implied such a statement. Eve was sucked into the Devil's deception because she too, added to God's Words in *Genesis 3:2* when she said **"neither shall ye touch it"**. To me, the principle of adding to the Word of God seems to be more criminal than the principles of subtraction or addition, but notice the admonition in *Revelation 22:18,19* **"For I testify unto every man that heareth the words of the prophecy of this book, If any man SHALL ADD unto these things, God shall add unto him the plagues that are written in the book: And if any man SHALL TAKE AWAY from the words of the book of this prophecy, God shall take away his part out of the book of life, and out of the holy city, and from the things which are written in this book"**. Jesus said in *Matthew 5:19* **"Whosoever therefore shall break one of these least commandments AND SHALL TEACH MEN SO, he shall be called the least in the kingdom of heaven..."** These modern translations teach men to break the commandments of God because they remove many of His Words. Jesus placed strict importance upon every one of God's Words in *Matthew 4:4* **"It is written, Man shall not live by bread alone, but BY EVERY WORD that proceedeth out of the mouth of God"**. The technique of dynamic equivalency is diabolical because it subtracts, changes, and adds to God's Words.

The transmission of words in a translation is vitally important. For example, we know the importance of getting a story right. If, in your absence, somebody said something, you would not know exactly what was said unless it was audibly recorded. Let's say you missed church on Sunday morning because your cat had the sniffles. In order to find out what was preached that morning you would have a few ways of finding out what was preached. You could either ASK someone or you could GET a recording. Which one do you think would be more accurate? To hear SOMEONES PERCEPTION of the message that was preached or TO HEAR THE ACTUAL WORDS THEMSELVES? Do you like your words taken out of context? This is exactly what has happened through modern translations. The technique of modern translators is simply their interpretation, perception, or their understanding of what a passage says instead of taking the actual Inspired Words that were spoken by God and allowing YOU to understand them.

The dynamic equivalency technique is very inconsiderate of the translators toward God. The modern translators are trifling with God's Eternal Word and do not respect His Kingdom. They make no effort to translate each word individually from one language to another. They translate it according to what they 'feel' it is saying. I do not want my Holy Bible to be based upon what some so-called expert FEELS that God is saying. I simply want God's Words as He intended for us to have them. How horribly corrupt are these modern versions! They are corrupted by using false texts and their technique in translating them is faulty – twice dead, plucked up by the roots. God's Holy Word is being tampered with by men of corrupt minds with carnal motives. How can someone have a proper perspective of God and His nature and how can someone have a right relationship with Him if they do not know the entirety of His Words? We base our experience upon the Word of God and if our Bible version is not complete then our experience with Him will not be complete. Our experience is to be based upon the Word of God, not the Word of God upon our experience or 'feelings' as these modern translators do. There are many verses in the Bible that warn us against subtracting from, changing, or adding to the Word of God. There are many references available that expose the multitudes of changes that the modern versions contain – these are listed in the bibliography.

THEOLOGY

In order for a contractor to build a house he must begin with the foundation. He then consults the blueprint to see what kind of materials he needs to build with. It is true that a house with a weak foundation will crumble, but it is also true that the materials make the house. If it is made out of hay or stubble it will be a weak structure and it will also be a fire hazard! Even if there is a good foundation, a good builder, and a good technique to build it – without good materials the house will not stand. The same is true with our Bible. The materials that are used to build a house are like the theology found in the Bible. Our King James Bible contains the purest theology; therefore man is able through the Written Word to have a right relationship with God. The modern versions, being corrupted, are theologically inferior to the King James Bible, and they will keep men from coming to the Truth.

Many, who are considered to be leading conservative/ fundamental scholars, have endorsed these false bibles and they make the claim that there are no doctrines affected. They claim that the theology in the modern versions has not been affected in any way; therefore there is no harm in reading them. In fact, you will be benefited by them because they are easier to understand. It is impossible to tamper with God's Word without changing the theology. For example, in the NIV, there is no mention of the **mercy seat, propitiation, sodomites, carnality, fornicator, advocate,** and many others. Every one of these words expresses some theological belief. Here are a few of the major doctrines that are affected:

<u>TRINITY</u> – *1 John 5:7, 8* **"Three that bear record in heaven, the Father, the Word, and the Holy Ghost, and these three are one"** is omitted in modern versions.

<u>ECCLESIOLOGY (Doctrine of the Church)</u> – *Revelation 2:15* **"Which thing I hate"** is omitted. Leaves us with the notion that Christ hates nothing, but it is clear that He hates iniquity and doctrines that destroy the Church.

<u>BIBLIOLOGY (Doctrine of the Bible)</u> – They completely omit or discredit *Mark 16:9-20*. They do the same with the woman taken in the act of adultery in *John 7:53-8:11*. I find it interesting that they omit the part of *Luke 4:4* where Jesus said **"Man shall not live by bread alone, but by every word of God"**.

They omit the phrase **"by every word of God"**.

There are many prophetical references that are confounded. There is a denial of the everlasting nature and fire of hell **(Mk. 9:46)**. There is also the denial of a literal heaven **(Lk. 11:2)**. There is a denial of salvation through the blood of Christ **(Col. 1:14)** and through Christ alone **(John 6:47)**. There is the denial that God was manifested in the flesh **(I Tim. 3:16)**. There is the denial of Christ's mission to save the lost **(Matt. 18:11)**. The deity of Christ is defamed by removing His title of divinity and reducing Him to the level of man. Many of these are removed from the text or they are discredited by a footnote that casts doubt upon them. For a more extensive list consult some of the resources found in the Bibliography. Hopefully, we are now able to see that Our Precious Holy King James Bible is superior to the rest in countless ways. May we cherish it and regard it with the highest respect and reverence knowing that men were willing to give their lives for its completion and God was willing to give His Son to show us its glories.

CHAPTER 9
DEVOTIONAL STUDIES ABOUT THE WORD
FROM THE WORD

A DESIRE FOR THE WORD OF GOD PART 1

"As newborn babes, <u>desire</u> the sincere milk of the word, that
ye may grow thereby:" *I Peter 2:2*

U pon reading this verse we must ask ourselves if we desire
the Word of God in this manner. It speaks of the
"sincere" milk of the Word. This means "pure" or
"unadulterated". It is the difference between skim milk and
whole. You can taste the difference and skim milk has less nu-
trients. These modern, corrupted versions are contaminated
and stripped of truth that is necessary for spiritual growth.
When you have been fed the pure, uncontaminated Word of
God you can tell a difference in the reading or preaching from
these false texts. If you have been truly born-again then you
will have a desire for pure truth.

The word "desire" means to "intensely crave possession of"
something. Have you ever seen a hungry baby? They will cry
louder and louder until they get your attention. You cannot
ignore the cry because they are determined not to stop until
you get the message – "I am hungry!" When that bottle of milk
finally hits their lips the crying stops and there is a sigh of re-
lief. Here we are told to desire the Word of God in this manner. Listen to the words of Job: **"Neither have I gone back
from the commandment of His lips; I have esteemed the
Words of His mouth more than my necessary food" (Job
32:12).** Job considered the Word of God to be more to him than

his physical survival. He had an understanding that man does not live by bread alone, but by every Word of God.

Do you have a desire for the Word of God? If so, to what degree does that desire affect you? Has it reached the intensity of a newborn baby's desire for milk? We must also ask, "Why do you desire it?" The text makes it clear that we are to desire the Word **that ye may grow thereby**. There are 2 things that are clear from this verse:

1. If you have been born-again you will have a desire for the True Word of God. Everything in the Word will satisfy your hunger – the promises and benefits, but also the rebukes and condemnations. You will desire ALL of it.

2. 2. You cannot continue to grow in Christ unless you drink of the Word of God.

If you do have a desire for the Word of God what are you doing about it?

Do you read the Word daily?
Do you meditate upon it?
Do you study it?

DESIRE PART 2

Peter said we are born again by the Word of God (**I Pet 1:23**). So, we have our _beginnings_ in the Word, but we are also _sustained_ by the Word. It is essential for us to remain in the Word of God to continue to remain in Christ. As for the newborn baby, he/she has a natural longing for milk. A baby does not have to be taught to desire milk. It is a NATURAL desire, an EARNEST desire, and a CONSTANT desire. The same is true for us. I worry about those who profess Christianity who have no desire to hear or read the Word of God. There should be an inner longing that constantly draws you to a private study of the Word – a longing that will not be quenched until you have read, heard, or studied it. We cannot ignore the baby's longing for milk. You can try to hold or caress them. You can try to distract them with toys, but they will continue to cry until they get the milk. As believers it is only natural that we would love the Word. The Christian's desire for the Word is also earnest and constant. Just as the baby must be fed if you want some peace and quiet – nothing should stop us in our pursuit for The Truth. The baby must be fed many times a day otherwise he/she will not grow. The same is true for us – we cannot make it on being bottle fed once a week by our pastor. This is the reason why we see so little spiritual growth. People have not learned to feed themselves throughout the week, and the world depletes their spirit of any vital power they received on Sunday.

If there is a healthy appetite that is fulfilled with healthy food there will be healthy growth. A consistent diet of Truth will promote growth. A diet of other things will promote carnality. There are hindrances to growth in the Christian life. We may see certain children that do not grow and there are only 3 possible causes for it. 1. There is a genetic problem 2. They have not been fed right. 3. They do not properly digest food. Now, in the Christian life there are those with a genetic problem. They have professed Christ, but never truly been born of the Spirit. There are also those who have not been fed right. They are not under the leadership of a pastor that preaches the Whole Council of God. They are fed only parts of Truth; therefore they cannot grow to Christian adulthood. In our day we see this case all around us – and the cause lies in the church's rejection of the King James Bible. People don't receive the entire Gospel – only a watered down portion of it. It is not 'the sincere' milk of the word. It is mixed with man's philosophies and vain babblings. There is also the problem of poor digestion. In our holiness churches many pastors preach the Truth, so the people are in an environment that is conducive to spiritual growth, but they do not digest it. It is not food EATEN, but food DIGESTED that makes us strong. Some people are like the picky, little child who will not eat the broccoli you put on their plate. They will eat just enough of the main course so they can get to the desert. Isn't that the way with many today? They want to possess the promise of heaven, yet they reject the necessity of walking the straight and narrow path to get there. One of the main reasons why people cannot properly digest the Truth is because they are filled with carnality. Notice *I Peter*

2:1 where **"LAYING ASIDE all malice, and all guile, and hypocrisies, and envies, and all evil speakings".** Before we can have a healthy hunger for the Word there some things that we must lay aside. You cannot have a proper desire for God's Word until these things are removed.

What is preventing you from having a healthy appetite for the Word of God?
What is hindering you from growing in grace?
What is hindering you from obeying the Word of God?

DESIRE Part 3

We have been talking about the importance of having a desire for God's Word. We must understand that man CANNOT LIVE on bread alone. I would like us to look for a moment at David's desire for the Word of God as expressed in that famed song which he wrote for the express purpose of magnifying the Word of God – *Psalm 119*. We will look at certain verses which express the intense desire that David had for God's Word.

v. 20 **"My soul breaketh for the longing that it hath unto thy judgements at all times."** What an intense expression of the strong longing in his soul. It was a gnawing emptiness that was only fulfilled by the JUDGMENTS of God. He would break for the desire alone – just to be in a place where God's Word was preached, just to hear some sweet refrain from the Scriptures, just to know more of the nature of God as revealed in His Word.

v. 32 **"I will run the way of thy commandments when thou shalt enlarge my heart."** This verse expresses desire. Running shows the earnestness and urgency behind ones purposes. You might remember when our Lord Jesus Christ had been buried in the tomb and had risen from the grave. The disciples, Peter and John, had been told by Mary that Jesus had risen and their first response was to run toward the tomb (John 20:4). The Bible says that John outran Peter. Could it be that his desire to see the risen Savior drove him to run with all of his might? Could it be that John's desire was greater than Peter's? Notice the text says "when thou shalt enlarge my heart". It is only proper to have such a desire when God enlarges or 'makes room' in our hearts. The problem is that often there is no room in our hearts for God's Word to take root. When we remove the useless clutter of this world we will make more space for the Commandments. Can you imagine how pleased God would be with us if we would RUN the way of His Commandments?

v. 36 "Incline my heart unto thy testimonies and not to covetousness"

Here David is asking for a desire. How often I've prayed for God to give me a consuming desire for Him and His Word. When you realize that your desires are not in the right place then it is only right to ask God to incline or direct your heart in the right direction. David expresses his desire to have his desires set in the right place and the reason why is because his desire was not always where it should be. Is it the same with you? We are not naturally inclined in the right direction. How often does covetousness get in the way of our desires. The desire for material or worldly things often causes us to miss our focus upon the eternal Word of God. Incline – or 'bend my will' in the direction of thy testimonies.

v. 72, 127 "The law of thy mouth is better unto me than thousands of silver and gold. Therefore I love thy commandments above gold; yea, above fine gold."

David was a king, yet God's law was more valuable to him than all of his wealth. God's law is valuable both monetarily and aesthetically because obedience to it always brings success. David was a king, yet God's law was more valuable to him than all of his wealth. David realized this; therefore his desire was set upon the law.

v. 82, 123, 148 "Mine eyes fail for thy Word, saying, when wilt thou comfort me? Mine eyes fail for thy salvation, and

for the word of thy righteousness. Mine eyes prevent the night watches, that I might meditate in thy word.

David's desire is here seen in his physical body. He ignores his body's desire for sleep because his desire to hear from God is greater. One of the best times to read the Bible is after the hustle and bustle of the day has died down and silence surrounds us in stillness of the night. David did this and sometimes he wept as he read the Word – Mine eyes fail. They pour forth tears of earnest desire to be able to accomplish what God asks in His Word.

Other verses for your consideration: *vs. 97, 113, 167* (LOVE), *v. 131* (PANTED), *vs. 136, 139, 158* (DESIRE FOR SINNERS TO KNOW THE WORD)

DELIGHT IN GOD'S WORD

We have looked at the importance of having an intense desire for the Word of God Now I want us to consider what it means for us to *delight* in the Word of God. It all begins with a desire. Then that desire is transferred to delight. It is the next step upwards in our relationship to The Word. Let's look at some verses in *Psalm 119* that express David's delight in the Word of God.

v. 16 "I will delight myself in thy statutes"

This word delight carries with it great emotion. It means "to please oneself" or "be amused with". It also means "I will skip about and jump for joy". Does the Word of God create that kind of feeling within you?

v. 24 "Thy testimonies also are my delight and my counselors."

Here the word delight means "enjoyment or pleasure" – "exceeding delightful". In other words, there is nothing quite as pleasurable to David as God's testimonies.

v. 35 "Make me to go in the path of thy commandments; for

therein do I delight."

He finds pleasure in that which brings pleasure to God. He finds his happiness in the Law of God. *Romans 7:22* brings out the fact that a righteous man delights in the Word of God. If you find pleasure or happiness in something then the chances are you will do it again. If eating chocolate brings you pleasure you will do it again. In fact, there is a possibility that you will over-indulge. You must practice moderation or it could reverse the feeling of pleasure by giving you a stomachache. The good thing about the Bible is that there is no such thing as "too much of a good thing". You can indulge yourself in the Scriptures and not be harmed.

v. 47 **And I will delight myself in thy commandments, which I have loved.**

You enjoy being with someone that you love. The more you love them the more you will want to be with them. You do not have to be forced to be with someone that you love. Delight is not a forced attitude. The word delight is an emotional word and it is closely tied to the word love as we are able to see in this verse. If you truly love the Bible you will spend time reading and studying. You will defend it when it is maligned. You will share its life changing power with those around you. I *John 5:3* says **"His commands are not grievous"**. They are not "burdensome" or heavy to bear. It is one of the strange misapprehensions of sinners that Christianity takes away more than it gives. It is true that there are things that we must give up to follow Christ, but it is also true that we receive much more in return. We receive peace, love, joy, a sound mind, a pure heart, and many more blessings too wonderful to describe, therefore we love God's Word. It gives life to us; therefore we love it and are able to love life.

George Mueller said "It is a common temptation of Satan to make us give up the reading of the Word and prayer when OUR ENJOYMENT is gone; as it were of no use to read the Scriptures WHEN WE DO NOT ENJOY THEM, and as if it were no use to pray when we have no spirit of prayer. The less we read of the Word of God the less we desire to read it, and the less we pray, the less we desire to pray".

David said **"I delight myself in thy statutes"**. I solace myself, refresh, recreate, rehabilitate myself in thy statutes. True happiness, delight, and enjoyment, can only be found when your heart is right with God. The Bible says **"In thy presence is fullness of joy, and at thy right hand there are pleasures forever more" (Ps. 16:11).** Jesus said **"I give you life, and that more abundantly" (Jn. 10:10).** The world's sense of pleasure is fleeting and temporary. It comes to an end eventually, but God's Word is a pleasure that is lasting. It continues to give pleasure to the righteous soul and it increases over the days and years. The Scriptures lead us closer to God; therefore they should be our delight. It is a wonderful thing to delight in God's Word. It is not a dead and dry experience, but we can have feelings about the Word of God. We can get excited about it. We can get excited about serving God. We can fall in love with the Bible. The Word of God is a sure cure for many of our troubles - Depression, Despair, etc... The Word of God will delight you if you love it.

Be careful of **DECLINING** from the Word **(Ps. 119:57)**

DWELL IN THE WORD OF GOD
**"Let the word of Christ dwell in
you richly in all wisdom..."** *Colossians 3:16*

The word "dwell" means "to inhabit". The word "richly" means "abundantly". It could read as such: "Let the Word of Christ abundantly inhabit you." If we dwell in the Word of God He will dwell in us. Israel only had God's presence abiding with them when the Law was present (in the Ark of the Covenant) and when the Law was EXALTED. The Shekinah glory dwelt in the innermost chamber of the Tabernacle and temple where the Law of God was contained. The Shekinah glory accompanied the Law. The two are INSEPARABLE.

The verse says **"dwell in you"**. In other words, "let the Word of God FIND ITS HOME IN YOU". Notice, it doesn't say "in your heart", but YOU. I am aware that David said **"Thy**

Word have I hid in mine heart" (Ps 119:11). The Word must first be put into your HEART where it is given the opportunity to take root and be able to produce fruit in our LIVES. Let the Word of God dwell in YOU – every part of you, not just your head or your heart, but ALL of YOU. Let it dwell in your mind, emotions, your mouths, and bodies. Let it INHABIT you or find its HOME in you. Some people are content to let him rent or lease the space in their hearts for a short period of time, but we need to invite Him in with intentions of letting Him inhabit our hearts as His home. Give the Word of God the privilege of owning every space of your life. Let it dwell IN you, not just lying on the surface like the seed that was sewn on the stony ground **(Matt. 13:20)**. Let it not be just a temporary entrance like the man who looked in the mirror and forgot what he looked like **(Jas. 1:22-24).** Let it be hidden **(Prov. 4:21)**, abiding **(Prov. 4:13),** and cherished **(Prov. 4:6-8)** in your life.

The verse also says "richly". Not a scanty portion. Is this the amount you have in storage? How can you be equipped to live a life that's pleasing to God without being filled to over-flowing with His Word? How can you have enough to give to others if you are not rich in The Word of God? Let it DWELL in YOU <u>RICHLY</u>. Let it be like a rich storehouse filled to capac-ity. Jesus said to the Pharisees in *Matthew 22:29* **"Ye do err, not knowing the Scriptures...."** Our failures, sins, and short-comings are there because we do not know the Scriptures, but continual cleansing with the Water of The Word will help us to correct them. Not only will these downfalls in our lives be cor-rected, but we will also be filled with true joy and peace. "Richly"- like the storehouse of the heart – *Matthew 13:52* **"Then said he unto them, Therefore every scribe which is in-structed unto the kingdom of heaven is like unto a man that is an householder, which bringeth forth out of his TREAS-URE new and old."** It is not my intention to expound upon this verse at this time, just consider its truths in conjunction with our study.

Look at the life of our Lord Jesus Christ. He showed us how a man full of God's Word should live. I understand that He is The Word, but as a man look how much of the Word dwelt within Him. If you were to do a study to see what percentage of His recorded speech was quoted from the Old Testament I wonder what it would be. He was constantly quoting Scripture in His sermons and in His everyday speech. Imagine as well, that when He was not quoting Scripture His very speech became the Scriptures that we now use. In what capacity does the Word of Christ dwell in you?

How can we let the Word dwell in us richly? Read, listen, meditate, memorize.

OPENED EYES

"Open thou mine eyes, that I may behold wondrous things out of thy law." *Psalm119:18*

$\mathfrak{I}$ love this verse – it has been one that I often pray. First of all, let us notice *verse 17*. It says **"Deal bountifully with thy servant, that I may live, and KEEP THY WORD"**. Now consider these two verses in their connection to one another. In order to keep His Word, we must first be able to understand it. This is a perfect prayer to pray before reading your Bible. It is implied that there are wonderful things to be found in God's Word, but we need the Holy Spirit to illuminate our minds so we can see them. It is also implied that there are things that we may miss unless our eyes are opened. Some say that what we need is a modern Bible, one with plainer speech that we may understand it. Others seek for new revelations and so-called prophecies, but what we need is God to open our eyes so we can understand the truth that He has given us in the Precious, Old, King James Bible.

A. B. Simpson used to tell the story of a poor Scotch woman who went to her pastor in her extremity, and told him of her poverty. He asked her if she had no friend or member of her family who could help her. She said she had a son, a bonny lad, who was in India in the service of the government. The pastor asked, "Doesn't he write to you?" "Oh, yes," she said, "he often writes me kindly letters and sends me such PRETTY PICTURES in them. But I am too proud to tell him how poor I am, so I have not asked him for any MONEY." "Would you mind showing me some of the pictures?" Asked the minister.

So Janet went to her Bible and brought out a number of BANK OF ENGLAND NOTES which she had placed there with the greatest care. "These are the pictures." The minister smiled for he realized she had money – lots of money – BUT DIDN'T REALIZE IT. The minister said to her, "Janet, you had a fortune in your Bible without knowing it."

Often, we too, are like that poor, old woman. We are endowed with such valuable riches – we are surrounded by wealth untold, but we do not recognize it. Those who neglect to read their Bibles will miss out on many of God's blessings. There are answers to life's secrets found in the Bible. Answers to the things that perplex and trouble us can be dug like gold out of a mine from the pages of the Bible.

The Bible is a closed book to the sinner and carnal believer **(Matt. 13:15, Acts 28:27, Eph 4:18)**. They don't even have a desire to read or understand it. When they do read, it makes no sense to them. But when you have been born of the Spirit you desire to read it and it is easily, effortlessly understood **(Eph 1:8, Matt. 11:25)**. But how often, even to us who are saved and desire to read it, do we find the Bible's precious truths passing us by. We gain a small nugget here or there, but we do not become wealthy in the Word of God. We are like spiritual paupers or beggars waiting for someone to hand us the goods instead of turning to the Holy Ghost and begging Him to OPEN OUR EYES **(Jn. 3:27)**. We stay at the same level we've been for years and do not receive new knowledge, but what could we become in the kingdom of God if we truly understood ALL that we have read? **"Understandest thou what thou readest?" (Acts 8:30)**. Some people feel as if they know everything there is to know about God and His Word – It is those for whom I fear. They are blind. Their eyes are closed and they do not see their need to have them opened **(Rev. 3:17)**.

Notice, the verse says **"wondrous things out of THY LAW"**. The Law? It refers to the Pentateuch. What kind of wonderful things can be found there? Some may say,"there are only rules and restrictions, and commandments that stifle my pleasure." But when your eyes are opened you are able to see that His Law is not just restrictions, but His Law is your Life! You will find joy in being obedient to Him. Even though His name isn't mentioned, you will find the Lord Jesus Christ everywhere in the Pentateuch.

Jeremiah 15:16 Thy Words were FOUND, and I did eat them; and Thy Word was unto me the joy and rejoicing of my heart.

THE HEARING EAR

"The hearing ear and the seeing eye, the LORD hath made both of them". *Proverbs 20:12*

𝕿 he previous study showed us the importance of being able to see; now we will look at the importance of being able to hear. It is vital that we hear the Word of God. *Jeremiah 10:1* says "**Hear ye the word which the LORD speaketh unto you, O house of Israel.**" There are many other verses which express the thought that we are commanded to hear the Word of God **(Deut 4:10; Josh. 3:9; Jer. 22:29).** But what do you do if you are deaf? How would you fulfill this command? It is a wonderful privilege to be able to hear. It is the Lord that has made possible this miracle we often take for granted – hearing.

How does the Word come to you and how do you hear it? Although we can hear it privately by reading out loud, it is often through speaking, preaching, or teaching that we hear the Word. We are more apt to hear it church, on the radio, or through some other medium. This is the way the Word comes to us. That's why *Ecclesiastes 5:1* says "**Keep thy foot when thou GOEST to the HOUSE OF GOD, <u>AND BE MORE READY TO HEAR</u>, than to give the sacrifice of fools.**" We need to understand that we need to put forth an effort to hear. When you go to church, prepare yourself to hear.

We will come back to this verse in a moment, but first I would like to look at *Matthew 13:15* which says "**For this people's heart is waxed gross, AND THEIR EARS DULL OF HEARING, and their eyes they have closed; lest at any time they should see with their eyes, AND HEAR WITH THEIR EARS, <u>and should understand with their heart</u>, and should be converted, and I should heal them.**" We must take this verse into context with that famed Parable of The Seed and The Sower which Jesus used to describe different classes of Bible hearers. There are key words and phrases in this verse which drive the point home that Jesus is making:

1. **"Understand"** – means "to comprehend" or "mentally put together"

2. **"Perceive"** – means "to know or become aware of"

3. **"Waxed gross"** – means "thickened with fat" or "calloused"

4. **"Dull of hearing"** – means "unable to hear" or "stopped ears" (Acts 7:57)

The ability of sight gives us the privilege of being able to see the works of Christ. The ability to hear gives us the privilege of hearing the Words of Christ. There is one thing about this statement that Jesus made that is clear: IT IS THE RESPONSI-BILITY OF THE HEARER TO UNDERSTAND THE WORDS THAT THEY HAVE HEARD AND ACT UPON THEM.

This takes us back to our verse in Ecclesiastes – **"Be ready to hear"**. There are certain reasons why we may not hear. We may be tired when we come to church. We may be bored. We may have selective hearing, or we may not have come ready to hear because there are other things upon our mind. All of these may be corrected and must be! If we are banking our whole lives on the Gospel of Jesus Christ we should give earnest heed to the words of the preacher.

During our study we have looked at the importance of having a proper translation to give us the UNDEFILED WORDS OF GOD. The modern versions are based upon feeling, or a man's commentary of what they think the Scriptures say. This is not to say that we don't need a commentary, but that is what our preachers and teachers are for. So, we ask the LORD to lead us to a pastor or preacher we can trust. We ask Him to place us where He wants us, so we can hear Biblically based preaching and teaching. This is why I do not condone many of the radio and television preachers of today. You will hear things that contradict the Word of God and the teachings of the Holiness Churches. Their teachings are hyper-Calvinistic, charismatic, and compromising. They will pull you away from the whole council of Christ. They will undermine our most precious doctrines of salvation, holiness, sanctification, Holy Ghost baptism, righteous living, and even the imminent return of Christ. This shows us the importance of having not only the pure Words of God, but a pure ministry from God as well.

Notice this verse in *I Thessalonians 2:13* "**For this cause also thank we God without ceasing, because, when ye RECEIVED the Word of God WHICH YE HEARD OF US, <u>YE RECEIVED IT NOT AS THE WORD OF MEN,</u> but as it is in truth, THE WORD OF GOD, which effectually worketh also in you that believe.**" How do you receive the preaching from your minister? Do you receive it as if it were coming from God? We tend to close our ears when certain ministers preach for a variety of reasons. Sometimes we've heard negative things about them. We may not like their style or mannerisms. They may hold to a slightly different standard or it may be that we're just plain stubborn and don't like to be told what to do. We must look beyond these things in order to hear and receive the message as if it were from God. I have been thoroughly blessed at times from the most unsuspecting people – I began to hear them with a bias, but as they preached, God's Word worked through them and touched my life. THIS IS THE REASON WHY WE SHOULD HONOR, UPHOLD, AND SUPPORT TRUE MINISTERS OF THE GOSPEL.

We should be ready to HEAR and cherish the teaching that we hear. We may wonder why certain folks may lack faith or struggle with worldly and carnal temptations when there have been volumes upon volumes of Truth preached from our holiness pulpits. There has been enough holy doctrine preached in our churches that would raise up a powerful army equipped to destroy the strongholds of Satan. Yet, how often does it seem that the gates of hell are prevailing against us? Do not take the preachers for granted. Do not take God's Word for granted – "**hear ye the Word of the Lord!**" (Jer. 2:4). Jesus gave us a parable to help explain the importance of hearing the Word. Do you realize that just because you go to church doesn't mean you will hear the Word? I have seen people in church defiantly resist the preaching of the Gospel. It is evident that they aren't receiving it. THEY MAKE AN INTENTIONAL EFFORT NOT TO LISTEN. On the other hand, there are well-seasoned believers who have come to church out of habit for years who may WATCH THE PREACHER PREACH, NOD THEIR HEAD, AND EVEN SAY 'AMEN' – WHO DO NOT HEAR THE WORD!

According to Jesus' parable you can tell if someone has actu-

ally heard the Word because there is a complete change in their life. Three classes of people in his parable (although there are 4 scenarios):
1. Those who are not changed
2. Those who are partially or temporarily changed
3. Those who are greatly changed. Which class do you belong to? There are those who hear it, yet don't understand it (Matt 13:19). We must PUT FORTH AN INTENTIONAL EFFORT to HEAR the Word of God and UNDERSTAND it. We must be physically ALERT, mentally ATTENTIVE, and spiritually ACTIVE when it comes to hearing The Word.

It is important to hear The Word. There are two basic reasons why:
1. It is necessary to CONCEIVE faith for your SALVATION (Rom. 10:14-17, Jas. 1:18, I Pet. 1:23).
2. It is necessary to CONTINUE in your SALVATION (I Tim. 4:16, II Tim. 3:14).

REMEMBER THE WORDS OF GOD

First we will look at *Jude 3* "....ye should earnestly contend for the faith which was once delivered unto the saints."
Jude reminds us of the importance of contending for the faith. In order to CONTINUE in our SALVATION we must CONTEND for the faith. One way that we do this is by remembering the Words of God. Notice Jude's admonition in *verse 17*: "But, beloved REMEMBER YE THE WORDS which were spoken before by the apostles of our Lord Jesus Christ;" There are many wonderful Words to remember that the Lord Jesus spoke as well as His apostles – these Words comprise our New Testament. Now, in Jude's case, he was speaking in particular about deceivers that would come in bringing false doctrines. This would cause people to FORGET the Words of God. Some Scriptures that our Lord and His apostles spoke concerning this matter can be found many places (Matt. 24:4,5,11,23,24; I Tim. 4:1,16; II Pet. 2:1,2; II Jn. 7-10 – just to name a few). These all mentioned the danger of being deceived by false prophets who would bring false doctrines.

The devil always bases his deceptions upon truth, and we have learned that he will deviate from it in the slightest degree in order to hoodwink us. It is important to HEAR The Word to CONTINUE in our SALVATION. In order to CONTINUE and CONTEND we must be able to distinguish truth from error. We must know The Word of God so when we do hear something that is contrary to it we will immediately recognize the difference.

5 WAYS TO HELP YOU REMBEMBER THE WORD

1. READ IT! *I Timothy 4:13* "Till I come give attendance to READING..."
2. HEAR IT! (Matt. 13: 1-23; Rom. 7:10) *Romans 10:14* "How then shall they call on Him in whom they have not believed? And how shall they believe in Him of whom they have not heard? And how shall they HEAR without a preacher?"
3. STUDY IT! (Acts 17:11, 12) *II Timothy 2:15* "STUDY to shew thyself approved unto God...."
4. SPEAK IT! (Eph 5:19; Col. 3:16) *Titus 2:1* "But SPEAK thou the things which become sound doctrine"
5. DO IT! (Ps. 119:17) *James 1:22* "But be ye DOERS of the Word, and not hearers only, deceiving your own selves"

SOME THINGS THE WORD OF GOD WILL DO FOR YOU:

1. Gives Faith – *Romans 10:17* "Faith cometh by hearing, and hearing by the Word of God."
2. Instructs in Righteousness – *II Timothy 3:16* "All Scripture is given by inspiration of God, and is profitable for doctrine, for reproof, for correction, for INSTRUCTION IN RIGHTEOUSNESS."
3. Sanctifies – *John 17:17* "SANCTIFY them through Thy Truth, Thy Word is Truth."

4. Comforts – *I Thessalonians 4:8* "COMFORT one another with these words."

5. Burns like fire – *Jeremiah 23:29* "Is not My Word as a FIRE..."

6. Breaks Apart like a hammer – *Jeremiah 23:29* "...and like a HAMMER that breaketh the rock in pieces?"

7. Reflects your true self – *James 1:23* "...a man beholding his natural face IN A GLASS."

8. Nourishing Food – *Jeremiah 15:16* "Thy Words were found, and I DID EAT THEM..."

9. Enlightens like a lantern– *Psalm 119:105* "Thy Word is a LAMP unto my feet, and a LIGHT unto my path"

10. Medicates for healing – *Psalm 107:20* "He sent His Word, and HEALED THEM..." It heals the spirit, soul, and body.

11. Protects like armor – *Ephesians 6:14* "...Loins girt about with TRUTH..."

12. Slices like a sword – *Hebrews 4:12* "For the Word of God is quick, and powerful, and sharper than any twoedged sword, piercing even to the dividing asunder of soul and spirit, and of the joints and marrow, and is a discerner of the thoughts and intents of the heart."

This is just a brief list of some of the wonderful things that God's Word can do for you. Now, consider how versatile it is and how useful it can be in the different situations we face throughout life. Also, consider these things in the light of our study on the various Bible versions. If the Word of God is described to be these things then how can the corrupted versions retain the same qualities? They will weaken the force of God's Word. For example, consider the Word of God being a sword. A sword is what ancient soldiers used for fighting on the battlefield. It was their offensive weapon used to destroy their adversary. We, as Christians must use the Bible as our sword to help us win the fight against the world, the flesh, and the devil. But what if that sword has not been sharpened correctly? What if it is dull and has only one edge instead of two? How will it do to gorge, gouge, and slice your opponent? The corrupted, modern versions have been made dull by removing the sharpness of God's Words. Is it any wonder, then, that many folks today who use these modern versions have no power against temptation and sin?

Consider, as well, the medicating properties of the Word. The Word of God is able to heal the spirit, soul, and body. When you have been wounded on the battlefield if you would apply the ointment of God's Word to your wounds it will heal you. Your spirit can be repaired. Your mind can be renewed. Your body is also a recipient of its redemption. But what of the modern versions? It would be like taking an aspirin for your aches, but never resolving the true problem. The True Word of God does not just treat the symptom. It treats the real issue at hand, but many folks today are not healthy spiritually because they have taken bad medicine. They have poisoned their bloodstreams with the venom of a man-made bible. When they come to these versions for help or healing they are not completely made whole. They are left half-healed or worse than when they came. But the pure Words of God are able to heal the sin-sick soul. His Words are able to solace the wounded heart. When you come to the "extra-strength" King James Bible and apply it to your life you WILL be made whole!

CONCLUSION

The purpose of this study has been to encourage us of the validity of the Bible – to encourage us in the fact that the Bible is precious, unlike any other book, because it is God-breathed. To increase our faith in it's promises, prophecies, and precepts, because the Eternal Father has spoken them. Another purpose of this study has been to help us give an answer to sinners and skeptics of the King James Bible. Skeptics need to be refuted intelligently. A 'because I said so' response will not be accepted. Many of us have been taught to rely upon the King James Bible, but we're not sure why. Hopefully, this study will give you some ground to stand on in your endeavors to convince the gainsayers. Remember, above all, to instruct them in a spirit of meekness.

For the most part, I have found that professed Christians are the gainsayers, skeptics, and opposers. They are the hardest to convince. Those who have been entrenched in this worldly church's philosophies are hard to convince of the truths of holiness, miracles, gifts of the Spirit, Sanctification, etc... In fact, most of them, have not even considered which translation is true. They accept whatever is given to them without even giving it a thought that there could be some discrepancies. This is one reason why we need to be familiar with our Bibles. We need to know it inside and out. We need to be familiar with its history and preservation. We need to be filled with its truths.

Granted, the critics will always find fault with the King James Bible. Yet, someone who has the ability to look at a subject honestly, without bias, will come to the conclusion that the King James Bible is the most perfect English translation. When people find fault with our Bible or our religion there are a couple of reasons why. It could be that they, being filled with darkness, are afraid of the Light. They are not willing to surrender all to Christ. It could also be that they have found a fault within our lives that contradicts the Truth that we claim to live by. Paul said in *II Corinthians 3:2* **"YE are our EPISTLE written in our hearts, KNOWN and READ of all men."** Our lives should be as flawless as the perfect translation found within the King James Bible. If we are going to defend the majestic Truth found within its pages then we need to live by it. People will not believe the Bible verses that we quote them unless they have first read the epistle of our lives and found it faultless. Let our LIFESTYLE be a perfect translation of God's Words. As we have looked at the corrupted translations and 'versions' of the Bible let our lives not be as such: subtracting, changing, or adding to the Scriptures. When people read YOU do they get ALL of the Truth or do they get a confusing, mixed up interpretation of God? Let us strive for perfection.

Let us hear the conclusion of the whole matter: Fear God, and keep His commandments: For this is the whole duty of man. *Ecclesiastes 12:13*

BIBLIOGRAPHY

Burton, Barry – *Let's Weigh the Evidence*, Chino, CA: Chick Publications, 1983.

Ergatees – *The Providential Preservation of the Greek Text of the New Testament*, Gisborne: Te Rau Press Limited (Pamphlet).

Fuller, David Otis – *Which Bible?*, Grand Rapids, MI: Institute for Biblical Textual Studies, 1993.

Gaebelein, Arno Clemens – *Listen! God Speaks,* New York, NY: Publication Office "Our Hope", 1937.

Gothard, Bill— Wisdom Worksheet (Booklet 19—Preliminary Edition)

Lee, Robert G. – *The Bible and Prayer,* Nashville, TN: Convention Press, 1950.

May, Herbert Gordon – *Our English Bible in the Making,* Philedelphia: Westminster Press, 1952.

Morgan, G. Campbell – *The English Bible,* Chicago: Fleming H. Revell Co., 1910.

Riplinger, G. A. – *New Age Bible Versions,* Ararat, VA: A. V. Publications, 1995.

Saphir, Adolph – *Christ and the Scriptures,* London: Morgan and Scott Ltd.

Scroggie, W. Graham – *Is the Bible the Word of God?,* Philadelphia: The Sunday School Times Co., 1922.

Scroggie, W. Graham – *What if There Had Never Been a Bible? (G. Campbell Morgan Lectureship),* Westminster Chapel: June 4, 1950 (Pamphlet).

Son, James – *The New Athenians,* Lubbock, TX: Praise Publishing, 1992.

Stock, Eugene – *The Story of the Bible,* London: James Nisbet & Co., 1906.

The Forbidden Book – DVD Video produced by New Liberty Videos, P. O. Box 25662, Shawnee Mission, KS 66225

Thieme, R. B. – *Canonicity,* Houston, TX: R. B. Thieme Bible Ministries, 1973.

Thomas, W. H. Griffith – *And God Spake These Words*, Philadelphia: The Sunday School Times Co., 1926.

Waugh, Thomas – *"The Clarion" or The Bible,* Joyful News Book Depot.

Waite, D. A. – *Defending the King James Bible,* Collingswood, NJ: The Bible For Today Press, 2004.

Waite, D. A. – *Foes of the King James Bible Refuted,* Collingswood, NJ: The Bible For Today Press, 2003.

Waite, D. A. – *The Case for the King James Bible,* Collingswood, NJ: The Bible For Today Press, 2001.

NOTES:

NOTES:

NOTES:

NOTES:

NOTES:

NOTES:

4392911

Made in the USA
Charleston, SC
13 January 2010